PRAISE FOR
GETTING GOOD WITH MONEY

"In the age of consumerism, Jessi brings calm into the chaos of living financially strapped by encouraging and guiding families to discover the beauty of living in financial freedom. No matter the size of your income, *Getting Good with Money* will lead you toward the stability you crave."

—ALLI WORTHINGTON, AUTHOR OF *STANDING STRONG: A WOMAN'S GUIDE TO OVERCOMING ADVERSITY AND LIVING WITH CONFIDENCE*

"Jessi has written a book so honest and vulnerable that it is sure to resonate with many working couples. Her willingness to get to the marrow of her own struggles lets the reader know immediately that she is in their corner. She is to the point, nonjudgmental, and offers practical advice applicable to real-life people wanting to get good with money. With a mix of heart and humor, Jessi is ready to guide readers on a better, more financially stable path."

—LYDIA SENN, HOST OF *FRUGAL DEBT FREE LIFE* PODCAST

"Jessi Fearon is a rare gem in the personal finance space. She has the unique ability to teach personal finance in a way that is encouraging, personable, and relatable. This book will change many families' lives for the better. I highly recommend it."

—CATHERINE ALFORD, AUTHOR OF *MOM'S GOT MONEY: A MILLENNIAL MOM'S GUIDE TO MANAGING MONEY LIKE A BOSS*

"Jessi is the real deal. She's been studying finance long enough to be an expert without being so far removed from money struggles that she's out of touch with how people going through them are feeling. Her empathy and encouragement will make you feel like you have a fighting chance at becoming financially secure, even if other methods haven't worked for you in the past. If you're looking for insight that goes beyond 'make a budget and spend less,' this is a book you're going to want to read cover to cover."

—JEN SMITH, CO-HOST OF *FRUGAL FRIENDS* PODCAST

Getting Good
with Money

Getting Good with Money

PAY OFF YOUR DEBT AND FIND A LIFE OF FREEDOM—WITHOUT LOSING YOUR MIND

Jessi Fearon

NELSON
BOOKS

An Imprint of Thomas Nelson

Getting Good with Money

© 2022 Jessi Fearon

Published in Nashville, Tennessee, by Nelson Books, an imprint of Thomas Nelson. Nelson Books and Thomas Nelson are registered trademarks of HarperCollins Christian Publishing, Inc.

Published in association with William K. Jensen Literary Agency, 119 Bampton Court, Eugene, Oregon 97404.

Thomas Nelson titles may be purchased in bulk for educational, business, fundraising, or sales promotional use. For information, please e-mail SpecialMarkets@ThomasNelson.com.

Scripture quotations taken from The Holy Bible, New International Version®, NIV®. Copyright © 1973, 1978, 1984, 2011 by Biblica, Inc.® Used by permission of Zondervan. All rights reserved worldwide. www.Zondervan.com. The "NIV" and "New International Version" are trademarks registered in the United States Patent and Trademark Office by Biblica, Inc.®

Any internet addresses, phone numbers, or company or product information printed in this book are offered as a resource and are not intended in any way to be or to imply an endorsement by Thomas Nelson, nor does Thomas Nelson vouch for the existence, content, or services of these sites, phone numbers, companies, or products beyond the life of this book.

This book is designed to provide readers with a general overview of budgeting principles. It is not designed to be a definitive investment guide or to take the place of advice from a qualified financial planner or other professional. Given the risk involved in investing of almost any kind, there is no guarantee that the investment methods suggested in this book will be profitable. Thus, neither the publisher nor the author assumes liability of any kind for any losses that may be sustained as a result of applying the methods suggested in this book, and any such liability is hereby expressly disclaimed.

Library of Congress Cataloging-in-Publication Data

Names: Fearon, Jessi, 1986- author.
Title: Getting good with money: pay off your debt and find a life of freedom—without losing your mind / Jessi Fearon.
Description: Nashville: Nelson Books, [2021] | Includes bibliographical references. | Summary: "Certified financial coach and mom Jessi Fearon leads the way for overwhelmed readers struggling to get a handle on their finances and lays out the doable steps her family underwent to pay off all their debts—even their mortgage!—and pursue their dreams, all on a $47,000-a-year salary"—Provided by publisher.
Identifiers: LCCN 2021007012 (print) | LCCN 2021007013 (ebook) | ISBN 9781400226108 (paperback) | ISBN 9781400226115 (epub)
Subjects: LCSH: Finance, Personal. | Finance, Personal—Religious aspects—Christianity. | Consumer loans. | Debt.
Classification: LCC HG179 .F377 2021 (print) | LCC HG179 (ebook) | DDC 332.024/02—dc23
LC record available at https://lccn.loc.gov/2021007012
LC ebook record available at https://lccn.loc.gov/2021007013

Printed in the United States of America

21 22 23 24 25 LSC   10 9 8 7 6 5 4 3 2 1

In loving memory of one of the greatest men in my life, my daddy. Thank you for teaching me how to always be willing to give to others even while in dire straits. You showed me what it means to work hard for what you have and to make the most out of what God gives you. I can't wait to see you again! AMDG (Ad maiorem Dei gloriam).

Contents

One

ENOUGH IS ENOUGH!

The day I hit rock bottom was March 3, 2013.

It was a rare spring day here in Georgia—the kind that is warm enough to wear a T-shirt but cold enough to wear jeans. I remember it clearly. While watching my one-year-old son play on the driveway with his monster trucks, I sat down to write out what we expected our expenses to be in just a few months when our second son was to be born.

As I looked over those numbers, my stomach churned. We were broke! As in, I-wasn't-sure-how-we-were-going-to-be-able-to-afford-diapers broke. You see, just a few months before, my husband had been in an accident, ending in an emergency surgery that wiped out our savings. Around the same time, the payment for my student loans started. I was a stay-at-home mom—something my husband and I both wanted for our family—but the reality was clear. If we didn't boost our income or reduce our expenses, we were in serious trouble.

Feeling lost and scared, I began to cry. How had this happened? After all, I was the one with the accounting degree! How would I explain to my husband that I'd failed us—that I couldn't make the money work? And worse yet, what happened if he felt like a failure because he didn't make six figures a year like some of his friends?

What about you? What is your current reality? Are you living paycheck to paycheck? Are you so deep in debt that you wonder if you'll ever get ahead? Does most of your income go toward making monthly payments for your house, cars, and credit cards? Or do you have enough money saved that if you or your spouse lost your job you'd still be able to pay your living expenses for a few months while searching for another job? Do you have enough money saved to retire one day?

What if:

- You could walk into a dealership and pay cash for a new-to-you car instead of having to finance it?
- You could take the mortgage payment you make every month and, instead of sending it to a bank, put it into your savings account?
- You could go on vacations without worrying about how to pay the bills when you got home?
- You could easily pay cash for a major car repair?
- You could give an unexpectedly widowed mother

money to help bury her husband without fear of
not having enough money to cover your own bills?

Today, this is my family's reality—but obviously, it is not
how we started. We really can walk into a dealership and pay
cash for a new-to-us car (and have now done it a few different
times). We now take our mortgage payment every month and
put it into our savings and retirement accounts rather than
giving it to Wells Fargo, because we outright own our home.
In six years, we went from being in debt to the tune of $55,000
to enjoying a net worth of over $300,000 as young thirtysome-
things with three children and a dog. And we did it all on my
husband's income of $47,000 a year.

We aren't rich. But we are free—free to make choices about
our life, free from worry, free to give. Being financially free is
better than I could ever put into words. But before we could
be free, we had to face some hard facts. If you picked up this
book, you are probably wondering how we did it and whether
or not you could achieve the same thing. And I'm here to tell
you that, yes, you can.

What Kind of Life Do I Want?

That life-changing spring day, I took an honest look at our
lives. I had no problem going back to the corporate world and
earning an income again. But I did have a problem with the
fact that most of my paycheck would be going toward day care

for two kids under the age of two. I also had a problem with the fact that living in metro Atlanta meant dealing with a lot of traffic every single day.

At the time, my husband, Pat, worked a job that didn't have a steady, reliable schedule. Some days he was home before dinner, while other days found him working third shift. At other times he worked out of state for months on end. This meant that if I did go back to work, the burden of working and driving two small children to and from day care would fall squarely on my shoulders. I envisioned my frantic self, rushing to get me and my two kids out the door in the morning. I could see myself fighting traffic just to get to the day care center and then fighting it again to get to work. After a long day at the office, I would have to fight the same traffic once more just to go pick up my babies. I could even hear myself cursing at the driver who cut me off as I tried to make my way home. The chaotic pace would only continue when I arrived home: getting kids settled, attempting to cook dinner, eating dinner, cleaning up after dinner, doing bath time, saying bedtime prayers, and then restarting the whole process again in the morning.

I hated every bit of that image. I don't like chaos. I don't like to be in a rush. I like to be on time, and, as all parents know, it can be a challenge to get kids in the car and out the door on time. I like peace. I don't like frantic.

For me, everything about that scenario made it very clear to me that we were about to be living a life we didn't want. We had envisioned a life of simplicity—one where, when the school nurse calls to tell you that your sweet boy is sick, you have the freedom to drop what you're doing and go get him. This crazy, chaotic life that I was now looking at was not the life either of us wanted.

What about your life? Does your life ever feel disordered? Does it seem so fast-paced that you feel as though you're constantly out of breath and forgetting little details? Too often we get sucked into the "more is better" mentality, and we think success means working sixty-plus hours at a job we don't love in order to pay for all the stuff and experiences everyone else seems to enjoy. But that doesn't sound very dreamy, does it?

When Enough Is Enough!

For us, our "enough is enough" moment came when we realized that the life we were trying to build for our family was about to slip away from us. But your "enough is enough" moment may look different from ours. Maybe that moment came when you couldn't pay for a simple car repair, or when you unexpectedly lost your job, or when your card was declined at the grocery store. An "enough is enough" moment is that moment of peak frustration, peak realization, a moment when you decide that something needs to change, something needs to give, because you will no longer accept living with the reality that stares you in the face—and change is the only positive outcome.

The truth behind managing your money better is that it's 20 percent math and 80 percent behavior. Meaning that if you truly want to make positive changes when it comes to money, you're going to have to change the behavior that got you there in the first place. If you've been on this earth for longer than a day, you already know that changing behaviors and habits is one of the hardest things we humans can try to do. It's hard to go against the grain. When "everyone" is in debt, debt seems natural and inevitable. But it doesn't have to be.

This is why you need to know *why* you want to embark on this amazing journey to manage your money better. You need to know why getting good with money is important to you, because when your old habits and comfy behavior start creeping up on you, you can quickly remind yourself why you wanted to do this, why you wanted to change, why you wanted to live differently than your peers and relatives or from consumer culture in general.

Living the Dream

Ask yourself this: When it comes to the dream life I want to live, what does that entail? Some people define it strictly in material terms—in the successful careers they have, the money they make, and how much they spend and what they spend on every year. We've become slaves to the "consume, consume more, and then consume even more" treadmill. We go to work just to earn barely enough to pay for all that consuming. The biggest struggle is that the consuming doesn't stop there. After we've paid the minimum payments on our debts, we take on more debt so we can consume even more. We don't want to be discontent, but we fail to realize that the person making us discontented is ourselves.

For example, when I became a mom, I discovered the convenience of Amazon Prime. It was just so easy to order what I needed without having to run out to the store. The downside of that was that I usually spent too much money buying things I didn't really need. And then, of course, shortly after making that purchase, there would be ads all over my Facebook and Instagram accounts advertising other items that were similar to the purchases I just made. Throw in all those influencers who make recommendations for the awesome products they use and, before I knew it, I consumed, consumed more, and consumed even more. I had bought into the material version of the dream life—the idea that the next "thing" I consumed would make me happy.

We have this perception that millionaires are rich, drive around in Lamborghinis, and live in homes that rival Buckingham Palace. Sure, some millionaires do fit that profile, but I discovered that most millionaires don't look anything like that. Many of them are average people, driving average cars, living in average homes, and working average jobs. These people have discovered the *true* dream life: the financial freedom to live their lives in a way that gives them peace of mind, contentment, enjoyment, and fulfillment.

In other words, the real dream life is the opportunity to pursue happiness in the way that suits you best yet also is within the realm of financial reality. My dream of a peaceful life at home with my kids may not be your dream. But discovering what *your* dream is will help you get off the consumer treadmill and move toward the life *you* want.

Part of my "enough is enough" moment—when I realized my life was not heading in a direction I wanted—was the lack of peace I felt. Sure, we could have continued on and I could have gone back to work in the corporate world. No one would have been the wiser. On the outside we probably would have seemed to have it all, despite living a life that left us restless and discontented. The truth is, we had to get uncomfortable and make some difficult decisions to achieve the dream life we envisioned. If you want to live your dream life, you're going to have to be willing to get uncomfortable and make those changes too.

So here is my challenge for you. Ask yourself: How does everyone around me define the successful life? Is that something I want? If not, how do *I* want to pursue happiness? What do I want my life to look like five years from now?

To show you what I mean, here are some examples:

- I want the freedom to pursue my dream job.
- I want to travel around the world.
- I want the freedom to drop what I'm doing and be present with my children.
- I want to live near family.
- I want to make purchases without fear or worry.
- I want to be content with what I have.
- I no longer want to have to (or my spouse to have to) work eighty-hour weeks.

- I want the freedom to use my time and talents in
  ways that aren't all about earning an income.

Having a moment of "enough is enough" isn't a require-ment to managing money well, but you need to know what your definition of success is and how you want to live your life. Knowing these will give you the *why* and motivate you into action.

If you are struggling to figure out what your personal dream is, think of what you want your life to look like five years from now. Write down today's date, five years from today, and how old you will be in five years. If you are married or have children, write down how old your spouse will be and your children's ages. Then ask yourself: What do I want our life to look like on this day, five years from now, when I am XYZ age? I have found this process to be incredibly powerful in helping me envision our future life and motivating me to make the changes I needed to make to get there.

I want to pause here a moment to address my single read-ers whose personal dream includes marriage and family. Even if "the one" has not yet arrived, you can still take steps that set yourself up to achieve that dream. Learning to manage your money better as a single person will teach you good habits that will carry over into your marriage, giving your family a healthy financial foundation to build upon. And even if the married-with-kids life isn't something you're dreaming about, it's still important that you take care of you. Learning to man-age your money well will set you up for a lifetime of success and allow you to pursue the passions God has placed on your heart.

I promise that if you keep *your* version of the dream life in front of you, you will be able to put in the hard work and sacrifice needed to achieve that dream. You will make a budget. You will cut your spending. You will have those tough conversations with your spouse. Maybe you will even learn to cook at home! As a result, you will go from living paycheck to paycheck to forgetting that it's even payday. You will free yourself from the chains of a job that is sucking the very life out of your soul. You will see the beauty of having the money to pay for those unexpected times when life hits you right in the face. You will have the joy of giving your money, your time, and your talents to others, because you aren't chained to debt and financial struggles.

You will get to experience the freedom and the true beauty of the dream, as *you* define it. You will no longer live in fear of money running out. You will get to live life by your own terms. Enough is enough. So let's take the next step and learn to manage our money better—together.

Let's Make Some Money Moves

1. What was your "enough is enough" moment or realization when it comes to managing your money? Write it down and journal your thoughts around this moment.
2. What dream did you get sucked into that does not suit you?

3. What is your personal dream for your future? What would you like your life to look like five years from now? Write it down, then post it where you will see it often. This will be the *why* that will motivate you to make the needed changes in your financial life.

Two

WHAT IS YOUR MONEY STRUGGLE?

That spring day in 2013, when I woke up to the fact that we were broke, wasn't the first time I'd realized I needed to get better with money. Like most young adults, that realization came when I graduated from college, took my first job, and tried to live on my own for the first time. I was clueless.

For many years I had no idea how much money I brought home every month, nor did I know how much I spent. Sure, I could tell you to the dollar amount how much my minimum monthly payments were for my rent, car, furniture loan, and various credit cards. But I wouldn't have been able to tell you how much I spent on groceries or eating out or on the mindless shopping I did on my lunch break. Nor could I tell you how much money I owed on my credit cards or how much I still owed on my car.

Money was a great big mystery to me. I saw all my friends looking like they knew some big secret to managing money, but I was way too prideful to ask them for advice. As it turned out, they were just as clueless about money as I was! We were a bunch of young adults trying to navigate first jobs, serious relationships, and all the bills that came with living on our own. We had no idea what we were doing. We thought we were going to learn this stuff in college, but the only personal finance advice I got from a professor was "Don't ever use your credit card to buy groceries."

It was too late for me. I was already swiping credit cards to buy groceries and gas for the car because my paycheck never lasted. I felt I had no choice but to swipe my credit cards to survive until I received my next paycheck. This wasn't just a paycheck-to-paycheck cycle; this was more like a paycheck-to-four-days-before-paycheck cycle. I bought fully into the "fake it till you make it" philosophy, and it wrecked me. I was facing a mountain of $11,000 in credit card debt and I was only twenty-one years old. I was terrified.

The Four Money Struggles

When it comes to managing money, our struggles can usually be boiled down to what's common for four types of people. I know, because in my lifetime, I have been all these types more than once. I have also learned from experience that these struggles with money usually happen as a result of the "mystery" of money. My hope is that, after reading about these four types of people, your struggle won't be so much of a mystery, because—trust me—you aren't alone.

The *Floater* is someone who is caught living the paycheck-to-paycheck cycle and feels like there is no end in sight. They feel as if every time they make any headway, something pops up and completely derails all the progress they've made. Have you heard of Murphy's Law? Murphy's Law states that anything that can go wrong will go wrong. For the Floater, it can feel like good ol' Uncle Murphy has moved in and taken up residence. The biggest struggle for the Floater is figuring out how to beat the paycheck-to-paycheck cycle that feels never-ending.

The *Daredevil* is someone who has little to no savings. This person may not be caught in the paycheck-to-paycheck cycle, but they struggle to pay for big expenses without going into debt because of their lack of savings. The reason they're called the Daredevil is because they cross the tightrope of life without any lifesaving cushion beneath them. Without a solid savings strategy in place, any financial fall is potentially fatal. As the expression says, the Daredevil is "one paycheck away from bankruptcy." If they lose their job or a major life crisis happens, the Daredevil will struggle to keep themselves and their family afloat.

The *Spender* is someone who struggles with controlling their overspending and impulse buying. Often, the Spender is someone who can score amazing deals on things but uses them to justify spending money they do not have. The money mystery for the Spender is the why behind their spending. Many Spenders are not even aware of how much they are spending every month and what they are spending on.

The *Avoider* is someone who does not plan for their future. The Avoider is caught in the grind of everyday life and struggles with saving for retirement and planning for their future self and family. They may have even lost sight of their dreams and their potential. The money mystery for the Avoider is seeing how they can realize their dreams by taking small actions today. Many times, the Avoider has become so bogged down with their everyday lives that they are oblivious to the potential destruction they may be causing their future selves.

Maybe you identified yourself in one of these archetypes, or maybe you even see yourself in more than one. When I was struggling with money at age twenty-one, I was all four of them. Yes, it's possible to be all four, but that doesn't mean all hope is lost. If I could overcome these struggles, so can you. However, it is important to identify our personal struggles with money. Once we have identified what they are, they are easier to overcome. So keep reading for some quick, preliminary tips on how to break out of your own particular money struggle, whatever it may be. Of course, we'll dig into more detailed tips in later chapters, but in this chapter, the goal is to get a sense of where you are and where you're headed.

Quick Advice for the Floater

I wish I could tell all the Floaters that stopping the paycheck-to-paycheck cycle is as simple as just making more money. But the reality is, it requires a little more work. However, the good news is that the solution to the problem is well within your reach.

The first step is to know exactly how much money you make every month, how much you spend every month, and what you spend it on. Don't let this overwhelm you. I know you already feel as though you don't have enough money, but you need to know the actual numbers. Not knowing those numbers is what is keeping you locked in your money mystery. You need to know where your money is going, and the only way to solve this mystery is to make a budget and stick to it. We'll talk more in depth about making and keeping a budget in the next chapter. Your first step for now is to keep track of your spending.

Look through your last thirty days of bank transactions and credit card statements. If you're primarily a cash spender, hold on to your receipts for the next thirty days. (You can use a sandwich bag kept in your car or purse to store them.) Then categorize your transactions and tally them up so you know how much you've spent and what you've spent it on in the last thirty days. Some common spending categories include clothing, entertainment, eating out, utilities, mortgage or rent, taxes, and so on.

Tracking and categorizing your spending is easier said than done, I know. But watching how you spend your money is a lifelong habit that you won't ever develop if you give up before you've even started. Over time, this habit of paying attention to your spending will forever remove that label of being a Floater.

Quick Advice for the Daredevil

Honestly, it's daring to live without any savings. I know from personal experience how scary it is to be hanging on by a thread and hoping that no unexpected bills show up in my mailbox. Everything feels overwhelming because you know you should have *something* in savings. But how much is enough? The big mystery for the Daredevil is not knowing how much to save or whether you're able to save anything. The Daredevil constantly lives in fear that one big emergency will pop up with no open line of credit available.

Having a solid savings account will save the Daredevil. You can't be a Daredevil anymore once you have a fully funded savings account ready to take on whatever life throws at you. And the peace of mind that savings account offers is incredible.

The first step for a Daredevil to overcome the money mystery is to make savings a priority. Daredevils will also need a budget, so be sure to read and follow the advice in the next chapter. The budget will help you find money to put into a savings account and create a safety net for when life happens.

If you don't already have a savings account or you don't yet have the minimum deposit to open one (typically $100), set aside five dollars in cash from your paycheck every payday, somewhere you won't see it and be tempted to spend it. Heck, give it to your mom if you know she'll save it for you. Slowly build up enough cash for the minimum deposit, and then head off to the bank and open a savings account.

Once you have opened an account, make saving money a habit. Don't get bogged down if you feel like you're not saving fast enough. Every little bit helps, and you'll be so grateful for it when the time comes that you need it. Notice I didn't say "*if* the time comes." That's because emergencies happen. It's not really a matter of *if* but *when*.

We'll dive deep into building up your starter emergency fund in chapter 7. For now, I just want you Daredevils to focus on building the habit of putting away money for emergencies.

Quick Advice for the Spender

Can we talk about a big weakness of mine? I care so much about what other people think of me. I know. I know you're not supposed to care so much about what others think of you, but I completely struggle with this. And it has led me down some dark holes in my life. Like the time I went on a massive shopping spree after a friend suggested my wardrobe needed to be updated.

It has led me to spend money to fix my so-called issues. But the trouble was that I didn't really have any issues to begin with, just perceived ones. Once I recognized my spending trigger, I was able to pull in the reins on all my crazy spending habits. And this leads us to the money mystery of the Spender: things that trigger impulse buying.

For me, Target is another weakness. Oh, my goodness, I can walk into Target for one thing and walk out with almost a hundred dollars' worth of stuff I don't even remember grabbing. I mean, I love Target. I love all the home decor pieces and the clothing and the fact that they have a Starbucks inside! It's enough to make me completely lose my mind, and it has on so many occasions. That's why, when I was on my debt-free journey, I knew I had to stop going to Target. I knew if I went inside, I would struggle to stay within my budget. So I had to remove the temptation altogether in order to keep myself from completely wrecking our budget. It wasn't easy. But it was worth it.

Once you know what your spending triggers are, you can stop yourself from pulling them. You won't be able to rein in your spending if you don't first do the heavy work of determining what triggers it.

Do you get excited when you see something on sale? It doesn't even need to be something that you want, just something that you see and immediately think, *Oh, Julie would love this!* And the good deal makes you feel like you should buy it right then and there. If so, then you know you have a "deal trigger," meaning you spend money when you see a good deal. The best way to combat this urge is to shop with only cash. Leave the card at home and shop with just the cash in your wallet, and only carry cash when you have a planned purchase like grocery shopping. You'll be less likely to spend money when you start to see how fast the cash leaves your hands.

Do you, like me, fall prey to temptation the moment you walk into Target? What about Amazon? Do you look things up on Amazon and find yourself all of a sudden needing this or that? If so, you struggle with a lack of clear priorities. I suggest writing down the items you need. For instance, a new work shirt because your current one is stained and you can't get the stain out. That's a need. But the cool new shoes or the latest bestseller is not. So get clear on your priorities before you go shopping, and you won't be as tempted to spend money you didn't plan to spend. In fact, I keep a sticky note on my laptop with a list of what we need to purchase. This keeps me from mindlessly shopping while I'm on my computer, and if I see a good deal on something that is on my list, I purchase it guilt free.

Quick Advice for the Avoider

I can't even tell you how long I was an Avoider. Maybe I thought I would never grow older. Maybe I thought I had all the time in the world to achieve my dreams and save for retirement. Who really knows? But what I do know is that the more you avoid taking action on your long-term goals, dreams, and saving for retirement, the further away you are from achieving them and the closer you are to being too late to start them.

Let me tell you a story about some friends of mine. This couple is beyond wonderful and I love them dearly, but they were classic Avoiders who ended up reaching retirement age with no retirement savings. And I mean absolutely nothing saved for retirement. They kept telling themselves that they would learn to budget and save their money, and that Social Security would be enough. But it turned out that $1,700 a month wasn't even close to being enough.

This amazing couple could not retire. They were deep in debt and struggling to make ends meet. They avoided saving for way too long. You don't want to end up in my friends' shoes. You don't want to be seventy-three years old and still having to work twelve-hour days. You don't want to sacrifice time with your grandchildren because you have to work the grave-yard shift. You want to be the grandma who bakes homemade cookies. You want to be the grandpa who lets the grandkids do things you'd never let your own kids do.

The big money mystery for the Avoider is figuring out what they want their future to look like and then putting that plan into action. It takes looking into your future and seeing what you want to have accomplished at the end of your life, and then bringing that vision back to the present. Once you do that, you can determine what your next course of action should be.

Remember in chapter 1 how I had you envision your life five years from now? If you're currently an Avoider, I would encourage you to picture your seventy-three-year-old self. What do you want to be doing then? Do you want to be sitting on your front porch, rocking back and forth, while your grandkids play at your feet? Do you want to be sitting on the beach in front of your condo? No matter how you envision yourself, I encourage you to take care of that seventy-three-year-old. That person is depending on you to make the hard choices and sacrifices now, so they don't have to when they've reached an age when working on their feet all day may be challenging.

Please know that if you're currently in dire straits and caught in more than one money struggle, you'll need to fix the other money struggles first, and then fix this one. So stop being a Floater, a Daredevil, and a Spender, and only *then* work on no longer being an Avoider. You'll find that the good habits you've gained in the process will help you face your future self with well-earned confidence.

Let's Make Some Money Moves

1. Identify your most pressing money struggle. Are you primarily a Floater, a Daredevil, a Spender, or an Avoider?
2. Review your dream for your future and consider how your current money struggle may be hindering you from achieving that goal.
3. Choose one piece of advice from this chapter that you most need to follow. Write it down.

Three

From Broke to Budget

Let's go back to my terrified twenty-one-year-old self who was facing a mountain of credit card debt, living in a way-too-expensive apartment, and driving a way-too-expensive car. I honestly didn't know how I was going to overcome my money struggles because everything felt so overwhelming. But I knew if I continued doing what I had been doing, nothing was going to change and I was just going to end up in further financial hell.

So I created my very first budget. It wasn't pretty. In fact, I just scribbled numbers on the back of a bank statement envelope. But those preliminary figures brought me face-to-face with just how dire my situation really was. Truth be told, I was running an almost thousand-dollar deficit every month! I knew things were bad before I made the budget, but I didn't know *how* bad. Once the budget was made and I realized what I had done, I was once again faced with a decision. I could run and hide and cry some more, or I could do something about it.

To be honest, I had no idea what I needed to do. I couldn't afford internet, and this was before the first iPhone came out, so I didn't have access to Google to help me figure it out. What I did know was that I could generate a little income by selling off some of my stuff. So I ransacked my apartment, categorized everything on my living room floor, and took pictures with my Fuji camera.

The next morning, I went to my mom's house to use her internet and uploaded the photos and listed them on eBay and Craigslist. By the end of the week, I had made a little over $150, which was enough to put a good dent in my smallest credit card balance. That was enough motivation for me to keep going. I sold more stuff and even took on a second job as a waitress. During this time, I also decided to go back to school to finish my degree, in hopes of earning more money from my regular job. To say that I hadn't fully bought into the whole debt-free lifestyle yet would be an understatement, since that degree cost me almost $30,000 in student loans.

Through this process of creating a budget and generating more income by selling things and getting a second job, I started to change my money story. I started becoming the financially responsible adult I had always wanted to be.

The Quick-Start Budget

So, what was this mysterious budget of mine that helped me realize how bad things were and propelled me to act? It was nothing special, but it was simple, and that worked for me.

I call this budgeting method the quick-start budget, because it gets you started with budgeting and will help you break the cycle of living paycheck to paycheck. In my opinion, this method helps to make budgeting "click," especially if you've never budgeted before. That's because we're going to be using your real money—as in the money you have sitting in your bank account. We're not going to be forecasting or trying to plan out a month's worth of expenses here. We're simply going to budget the money you already have.

Here's why I like this system:

- It's practical.
- It's easy to implement.
- It puts you in the driver's seat with your money (and your life).
- It's simple.
- It's an active approach to managing your money.
- It helps budgeting make sense.

Here's what you need to set up this budget:

- Your current checking account balance
- Your calendar

- Your preferred place to keep your budget (spreadsheet, piece of paper, etc.)
- A calculator

Here's what you're going to do. Take whatever balance you currently have in your checking account and then subtract all the bills that must be paid between now and the next time you get paid. Once you've done that, subtract how much you'll need for groceries, gas, and any other expenses until your next paycheck. Also make sure to account for any transactions that have not hit your checking account balance, like the check you wrote for your child's preschool tuition.

Below is how this might look on paper:

- Checking account balance: $1,000
- Bill 1: $150
- Bill 2: $70
- Bill 3: $65
- Total remaining: $715

This $715 is what you have to budget for groceries, savings, and other life expenses. Below is how it can be broken down:

- Groceries: $200
- Savings: $100
- Tithe: $100
- Gas: $85

- Haircut (including tip): $50
- Eating out: $75
- Mom's birthday gift: $30
- Christmas fund: $75
- Total remaining: $0

This is called a zero-balanced or zero-based budget, where every penny is given a job and assigned to one category or another.

Don't get lost in this example; it's merely an example and not a representation of the numbers you will be working with. Your numbers and your categories are going to look different.

While most personal finance gurus may tell you to "pay yourself first" by putting money into savings, I want you to pay your bills first. If you've never created a budget before, coming up with a reasonable and doable number to save is going to be a bit of a challenge. So for now I want you to start off with what you do know: your bills. Then later, work your way toward how much you can set aside for savings and tithing.

With that said, though, I still want you to save something each month because it's crucial and essential to your overall survival and financial health. Even if you are struggling to make saving money a priority right now, I encourage you to keep it as a line item in your budget. And even if it is only five dollars every paycheck, it's something.

I know this quick-start budget probably looks different from the ones you're used to seeing, but I think it's a great place to start, especially if you've never created a budget before. As you get more and more comfortable with budgeting, work to live by your monthly budget instead of living paycheck to paycheck.

Maybe you need some help visualizing how a quick-start budget (or any budget for that matter) can help you. Maybe you're still caught in the belief that you'll budget "when you have money" or that budgets are for broke people. If that's you, I want to encourage and challenge you, because honestly, without knowing where your money is going, you'll never be able to achieve all the success you're capable of.

Do you have student loans or maybe even a wedding loan you'd love to see paid off one day? Do you want to be able to save for a down payment on a home? Do you want to be able to take vacations that are free of money worries? Is there a charity you wish you could afford to support? Do you just want to be able to pay for day care without worry? Do you wish your spouse was interested in the finances of your home? If so, the only way you'll ever achieve those ideals is if you learn how to manage well the money you do have.

Sinking Funds

There's a little-known secret in the world of personal finance that can dramatically improve your budgeting efficiency and help you keep a positive cash flow. *Sinking funds* are separate funds where you set aside money for an intended purpose. Our family uses separate bank accounts for these kinds of expenses. They are called sinking funds because of the accounting term "sunk costs," which are costs that have already been incurred and cannot be recovered—thus, they are sunk. Sinking funds are very similar in concept: you're saving money to use at a later time for a specific purpose but treating it as if you've already spent it; that is, the money cannot be recovered.

We have sinking funds for auto-related costs, such as new tires, oil changes, and other regular car maintenance; Christmas; vacations; home maintenance; and medical costs (we're not eligible for an HSA or FSA). If you find that your household finances are regularly being upended when something like a dead car battery happens, set up an auto sinking fund. That way, the money doesn't need to come out of your household's quick-start budget. This is also a super easy way to budget for Christmas (and other gift-giving moments) and vacations, because whatever amount you've saved in your sinking fund is your budget. No more guessing—and then going over—your Christmas budget every year!

The Key to Success: Building Smart Habits

The key to the quick-start budget method is that it builds smart habits. If you've always struggled with sticking to a budget, this method will get you in the habit of actively paying attention to your money. If you get paid every two weeks, know that you're going to be looking at your budget and your money at least every two weeks. Granted, you should look at your money more often than that, but this is a start.

Every time you get paid, add your current paycheck amount to the balance of your previous budget from your last paycheck. Repeat the process of looking at your calendar, listing all your upcoming bills and expenses, and then doing the math to determine if your budget is balanced. This way, your money is always in front of you. You will know where your money is going and have a plan for it.

Ending the Cycle

Stopping the paycheck-to-paycheck cycle is not easy. If it were, no one would ever find themselves stuck in this cycle. This means you're more than likely going to run into some bumps in the road as you attempt to gain control over your money. On average, it takes about three months of consistently budgeting for it to become second nature. Give yourself grace. Making your quick-start budget and following through with it is challenging in the beginning. It's hard to try new things and change old habits. The key to making this whole thing work is to keep going even when things get tough.

To make sure you keep your budget in check, the next step is to determine what expenses are important to you and what are not. Now, if you're in the same situation as I was at twenty-one, you probably already realize that you can't spend any money on things that aren't essential right now. If that's you, know that this is just a season of your life, and you can work your way out of this season by tracking your expenses and budgeting.

If you have more wiggle room in your budget, you may have more discretionary spending, which is fine. Just make sure you have an emergency fund in place. We'll talk more about emergency funds in chapter 7.

A Quick Word About Tithing

I'm from the South, otherwise known as the Bible Belt, where as soon as you introduce yourself, you're asked what church you attend. Down here, tithing—as in giving the church you attend 10 percent of your income—means a lot. Like if you told people you weren't giving that full 10 percent (and it'd better be 10 percent of your gross pay, not take-home pay), they would probably pull out their Bible app and recite Leviticus 27:30 or Proverbs 3:9 in a full-on guilt trip.

This is probably where I differ as a Christian, because I was raised in a church where we were taught to always pray before giving. I didn't grow up with the strict belief that I must give exactly 10 percent of my income, and I know that my fellow Christians may disagree with this. However, I have always held to the belief that I need to live and give in accordance to how and where God calls me.

My husband, Pat, was an atheist when I married him, and he was completely against tithing. Now he's a baptized Christian, and even though he still struggles with the idea of giving money to a church, we give to ours. But while we were on the debt-free journey, Pat was not a fan of tithing. He believed that we needed to free ourselves from the chains of debt quickly, and then discuss tithing. Honestly, this whole debate caused a lot of friction in our marriage. I was angry about it and took the whole thing to God in prayer. Through prayer, I understood very well that God wanted me to let go of giving to the church, and instead put a prayer request in the offering basket.

I share this with you because, if you find yourself in a situation where either you simply do not have any money to give to your church—10 percent or not—or you're struggling with this idea, I want to encourage you to pray about it. I can't tell you what you should or should not be giving to your church; only God can.

I know that this may make me seem like a heathen to some because I'm not pushing that tithing is a must. But the reality is, I am not God and I cannot tell you what you should do with his money. Jesus warns us in Matthew 23:23 against focusing too much on the rules of tithing without paying attention to the more important things like faithfulness, mercy, and justice. Even if you dutifully give 10 percent of your gross income to your church, I would still encourage you to take your offering to the Lord in prayer. You may be surprised by what he asks of you.

Prioritize Your Expenses

When it comes to getting your budget balanced, you're going to have to determine which expenses are important to you and which ones are not. To me, living a real life on a budget all comes down to knowing what you want to spend your hard-earned money on and what you don't.

To do this, list your priority expenses. What bills are the most important to your family? The obvious ones are, of course, your rent or mortgage payment, taxes, utilities, and food. After those, which discretionary expenses most contribute to the well-being of you and your family? For help, think back to your own particular vision of the dream life. Then look over all your expenses with a critical eye. With each expense, ask yourself: Does this help me achieve that dream?

For example, my dream was to be a stay-at-home mom. It soon became obvious that eating out and taking expensive vacations would prevent me from living that dream. So I eliminated those expenses, hoping my short-term sacrifice would lead to my long-term satisfaction. It did. And it will do the same for you.

Perhaps your dream is to own a home or the exact opposite, like having the freedom to travel. Does your gym membership allow you to achieve that dream? How about all the streaming subscriptions you pay for? I'm not arguing that you will need to cut every little thing from your spending. I am saying that you should make sure you're not spending mindlessly on things that don't truly matter to you.

Here's where you're really going to have to battle against the cultures of YOLO (you only live once), FOMO (fear of missing out), and reality TV that sells you an ideal of what it looks like to have money. Your income is your greatest wealth-building tool. So if you spend it all, you won't have any left over to build wealth. Right? I know that seems obvious, but the reality is we often mindlessly spend our money. It's important to spend our money wisely and in accordance with our overall dreams and goals. As Jesus said, "Watch out! Be on your guard against all kinds of greed; life does not consist in an abundance of possessions" (Luke 12:15). Life is so much more than a flashy new wardrobe, an Instagrammable vacation, or the latest "great deal."

The key to budgeting is in knowing where you're spending your money. This is true whether you are a saver or a spender. Where we spend our money matters. When we're trying to reach big goals—savings goals, debt payoff goals, or retirement goals—the way we spend our money directly affects how quickly we will achieve those goals. This is why we must define our true needs and wants. Not being able to differentiate between the two is one of the biggest reasons we struggle to make any headway financially.

This doesn't mean that you must live uncomfortably. It just means you need to get very clear on what is important to you and what is not. Without this clarity, you'll struggle to gain any momentum in reaching your overall goals.

Eliminate or Reduce Expenses

Once you've listed out which expenses are a priority, you will need to go through all your other expenses and determine which ones can be eliminated or reduced. Now, with the extra wiggle room you created in your budget, you can find a new "home" for that money. You could use it to pay off debt, put it into an emergency fund, save it for a new car, or set it aside toward your retirement. It is totally up to you. I would suggest putting your extra money toward just one of these goals and making this goal a priority in your budget. Then once that goal is achieved, you can move on to achieving the next goal on your list.

Here's a suggestion on how to determine which expenses to eliminate or reduce. Ask yourself if the expense is one that you can live without—at least temporarily. If it is something you can go without for a while, eliminate it. Typical expenses that can be *eliminated* include:

- Entertainment, such as concerts, plays, and sporting events
- Dining out
- Extracurricular activities for the kids
- Vacations
- Cable and streaming services
- Expensive hobbies

If it is something you can't live without—like groceries— ask yourself if there are potential ways to reduce this expense.

Typical expenses that can be *reduced* include:

- Groceries
- Utilities
- Insurance premiums
- Internet
- Phone service
- Rent or mortgage payment

When it comes to reducing your expenses, sometimes it's as simple as a phone call to your current provider to see if they have any promotions that would reduce your monthly bill. Other times, it may require a little more legwork. I suggest, when trying to find a cheaper provider for things like insurance, you call an independent agent, since they can gather quotes from various insurance providers to help you find a less expensive policy. If you work from home, see if your employer would be willing to pay a portion of your internet bill. If you own your own business, talk to a CPA about having your business pay for a portion of your internet or cell phone bill through an accountable expense reimbursement plan.

For us, putting our quick-start budget into action was both freeing and a little intimidating. We loved the ease of figuring out the flow of Pat's paycheck for the week, but we didn't really see eye to eye on the expenses that needed to be reduced. I was willing to go with the cheapest insurance policy and provider there was. However, Pat is a staunch believer that "you get what you pay for" when it comes to insurance.

Needless to say, he was not willing to budge on insurance. So we had to find a compromise. Pat was willing to negotiate with our current provider to find us the best rate without sacrificing our current policy, and he agreed to give up eating out for lunch to afford it.

This was just one of the many compromises we had to make during our financial journey. Don't fret if you and your spouse don't see eye to eye on the expenses that need to be eliminated or reduced. Work to find a compromise. You're a team, and teams work together for the common goal.

Sometimes the best thing you can do for your budget is to be aware of how much you're spending and whether you're spending on things that truly matter to you and your family. Remember, budgeting doesn't need to be complicated. The simpler the better when it comes to managing your money. So, if you haven't already created your budget, now's the time to do it!

Let's Make Some Money Moves

1. Ask yourself: Is the current way I manage my money bringing me closer to the life I dream of? If not, ask yourself why and what changes you need to make.
2. Write out your quick-start budget. This does not have to be fancy. You can write this in a notebook or put it in an Excel spreadsheet. Don't feel like you need an expensive planner to do it.

3. Determine which expenses are a priority and list them separately, so you can keep them front and center.
4. Discover where you can eliminate or reduce expenses, then take action immediately on those expenses.

Four

What's Eating Your Budget?

Have you heard the expression, "The devil is in the details"? If not, it means that to avoid failure, you need to pay attention to the details. But there is a much older saying that I believe carries more weight: "God is in the details." This expression means something slightly different in that attention paid to the small things carries a great reward, or paying attention to the small things is how goals are achieved. Don't get me wrong—paying attention to the details to avoid failure is good too. Either way, a war is not won because of one battle; it is won because of a series of battles fought in succession. Attention to the small things will reap incredible rewards.

While we were on the debt-free journey we had to pay close attention to every little detail as we worked to free up our income from the binds of minimum payments. I had to ruthlessly cut our grocery budget and figure out how to feed our growing family on less and less money. Pat, who believes food that has sat in the fridge for longer than a day has gone bad, had to learn how to eat leftovers and enjoy them. We had to learn to look at the small details of our everyday life in order to reap the reward of achieving our debt-free goals. Likewise, you will need to look into the details—even those mundane, seemingly ordinary details—of your everyday life to determine where you can reap the most rewards. In other words, you need to figure out what's eating your budget.

Cutting the Grocery Budget and Not Starving to Death

My husband's nickname growing up was "Fat Pat." No, I would not consider my husband fat, not even back in high school. But that was his nickname because the man can *eat*. Because he's in construction, he burns through calories fast and needs more food than a lot of other guys his size. I don't think I have to tell you how this affects our grocery budget. I've had to learn through the years how to get creative to make sure our entire family is well fed and no one goes hungry.

I want to let you in on a grocery budget secret because it's important. When it comes to trying to figure out how much to budget for groceries, the question to ask yourself isn't "How much money will this food cost?" but "How much (or which) food can I buy with the money I have?" And then, of course, the next question is "How much money do I have for food?"

If you've already made your quick-start budget and have been working to make that budget work for you, there's actually very little guesswork involved in figuring out your grocery budget. For example, let's say you have $200 in your checking account and you just got paid today so the total in your checking account is $1,000. Using the quick-start budget method, you would first start with the bills that are going to be due before your next paycheck and subtract those out of the $1,000 balance. From there, you would budget the rest of the money for groceries, the starter emergency fund or debt payoff, fuel/ transportation costs, and so on.

One more note about groceries: please do not think your grocery budget must be a certain amount or a certain percentage of your income. You or a member of your household may have food allergies that bump up the cost, or you may live in a part of the country with a high cost of living and little access to low-cost grocery stores. It would be impractical to compare your grocery budget to others who can purchase foods without fear of harming someone they love or who have access to stores like Aldi. *You* get to pick how much you're going to spend on groceries every month. To start, just look over how much you've been spending on groceries. Then adjust your budget as you employ new money-savings tips.

If you make a quick-start budget, you'll know how much you can spend on groceries before you go to the store. This is super important, because you can't walk into the grocery store and spend $300 when you have only $150 left from your last payday. But don't stress if you find yourself in that position where you need to buy more groceries than you have money for. The steps below will help you make your grocery budget (no matter how small) work for your current financial situation.

STEP 1: LEARN TO COOK

Perhaps this is an obvious point, but if you don't regularly cook at home, your grocery budget can quickly be eaten up by costly convenience foods, such as frozen dinners, pizza, and takeout. You don't have to become a world-class chef to cook well. My suggestion is to make a short list of meals (about three to five) that you would like to learn how to cook. Look up recipes for those meals and try one—just one this week. Don't overwhelm yourself and try to cook every night if you don't regularly cook. Start with one night a week where you try to cook a new meal and build from there.

STEP 2: IF POSSIBLE, STOCK A PANTRY AND FREEZER

I don't have an actual pantry in my kitchen because my home was built in 1979 before those kinds of things were standard. But I try to keep a few staple items on hand. This keeps me from having to purchase them every week and allows me some flexibility in our meal plan. Some staple items I keep on hand are broths (chicken and beef), canned tomatoes, pasta noodles, and frozen veggies. For me, these are ingredients I use often and can be substituted in meals rather easily.

To make stocking up on these items fit into our grocery

budget, I will purchase one for now and two for later. In other words, I will purchase one carton of chicken broth to use this week and two for the following weeks. I do this until I have a modest stockpile, at which point I can forgo buying that item for a while. This allows me the flexibility in our grocery budget not only to lower it but to use the savings toward our current goals.

Step 3: Make a List of Favorite Meals

One of my best grocery tricks is to have a list of my family's favorite, easy-to-make meals. I use a baby-blue binder to store the recipes for these meals, along with an ingredient list. On days when I don't feel like cooking or when I think we don't have enough food in the house to make anything, I pull out this baby-blue binder and go over the ingredient list. Next to this list of ingredients I include different recipes that use that ingredient. Every single time I've pulled out that binder and taken a quick inventory of the ingredients I have on hand, I've found something to make that night for dinner. The best part is that all the recipes on that ingredient list are ones my family already loves! So there's no stressing over whether or not my family will enjoy it.

If you struggle often with not wanting to cook or simply not knowing what to cook, I suggest creating something similar to my meal binder. This doesn't have to be complicated. Just grab or print out all the recipes you've made previously that you know your family enjoys. It can simply be an ingredient list along with recipe names that you tack on the inside door of your pantry. I promise you this simple trick will curb all those nights of ordering takeout.

STEP 4: CREATE A MEAL PLAN FOR THE WEEK

For many people, meal planning can be more overwhelming than learning to create a budget. But it doesn't have to be, nor does it have to be strict. Just because you write out that Monday is supposed to be braised pork chops with mashed potatoes and green beans doesn't mean you have to actually make that on Monday. Maybe you had a difficult day and making that kind of meal is too much work. Enter that favorites list you made! Either make something from your family's favorites or make another meal you had planned for later in the week.

Here's my exact process for meal planning. I sit down and go over our calendar for the upcoming week, so I know how busy the days look. If our week is going to be super busy I immediately know I need to plan quick and easy meals. Once I know what our week will entail, I start writing out my meal plan. Although I assign a meal for each day, that doesn't mean we'll be eating exactly those meals on those days. I simply write them down by day to ensure that I've accounted for all the days.

I don't make a meal plan for breakfast because they are pretty simple around here. But if your family enjoys a more elaborate breakfast, definitely include it in your meal plan to make sure you have everything you need for those mornings! I also don't make a meal plan for lunches because we mostly eat leftovers for lunch. However, I do make sure that staples are on hand to make sandwiches should the need arise.

STEP 5: TAKE INVENTORY AND MAKE A GROCERY LIST

Now that you know what meals you're planning on having this week, it's time to take inventory. No, I'm not talking about the kind of inventory I used to have to do when I worked at Fashion Bug back in high school. You don't need to pull everything out of your pantry or refrigerator to do inventory (even though it's a great idea to do that every few months). But you do need to make sure you have what you need to make your meal plan work, as well as anything else your family may be out of.

You may need to take note of the things you do *not* need to purchase on this shopping trip. For example, I usually buy two cartons of half-and-half for our morning coffee. But sometimes we actually have too many cartons in the fridge. In that case, I don't need to purchase any on this shopping trip because if I did, I would only be adding to a hoard of half-and-half I already have, and eventually they're going to go bad faster than we can use them up.

There is something else you need to think about before you head off to the store: Do you throw away a lot of food because it goes bad faster than you consume it, or do you need to make multiple trips to the store each week because you run out of things quickly? If either is the case, make a conscious effort to pay attention to what you're purchasing. Are you buying things you and your family actually like to eat? Are you buying enough or too much of the item?

At one point we were throwing out a lot of produce because it went bad before we could eat it all. This was around the time when we switched to a mostly clean, minimally processed diet, so I couldn't understand why produce wasn't being consumed. The truth was that we did eat produce regularly, but we didn't eat enough of it before it went bad. So I started purchasing those specific items frozen instead of fresh. This way they would last longer, and we didn't waste money.

If you throw out a lot of food because it's not being eaten, dig deep to figure out why. Is it because no one is eating leftovers or because your family simply doesn't like that item? No matter the cause, it's important to understand the *why* so you can remedy the issue. The same process applies if you are making multiple grocery store runs. Start tracking how much of the item your family is actually consuming so you can figure out exactly how much to buy each week.

As you take inventory, make a grocery list. This could be either a handwritten list, a standard updateable checklist, or a list created by an app. Experiment with a few strategies to find what works for you. If you don't like taking an extensive inventory, keep a running list, jotting down the items you need as you use them up. If you have a favorite grocery store, you might want to create a list that reflects what is found in each aisle—thereby reducing the number of times you have to consult your list as you shop.

Step 6: Keep a Price List and Make Substitutions When Prices Are High

To buy things on sale, you need to know what a "sale" is! And the only way to recognize a sale is to have a sense for what the regular price is for an item. Enter the price list. This is a list of your most common grocery purchases, along with the lowest amount you've paid for the item.

When you start out, you may need to make a formal, written price list. But as you shop more often you'll learn to recognize a good price almost instinctively. When the prices are good according to your price list, you may want to stock your pantry or freezer. Another idea is to substitute items when prices are high. So if you go to the store hoping to buy pork but find chicken on sale instead, buy the chicken. However, don't just buy something because it's on sale. If you've never tried the food before or you're not sure how to cook or use it, you're probably better off not purchasing it. You can almost always substitute a store brand for a name brand, and coupons may be entirely unnecessary if you shop at a discount store like Aldi.

Another thing to keep in mind when it comes to prices is that the cost per unit matters. A lot of people buy in bulk at Costco, thinking they are saving money, when in fact they might pay less for the same item (but not in bulk) when it's on sale at the local grocery store. Keeping a price list and checking the sales at your local grocery stores will guard you from paying more unnecessarily.

STEP 7: SHOP WITH CASH

I mentioned earlier that back in my college days, a professor told us that the number-one rule when it came to managing money was to "Never use your credit card to buy groceries." As she knew already, and I eventually found out, credit cards shouldn't be used for anything and everything. Money doesn't grow on trees, nor do credit card bills just magically get paid off.

I learned the hard way that the professor was right. Mindlessly swiping a credit card was a really dumb idea. But back when Pat and I were trying to figure out how to manage our money, I struggled with the idea of shopping with only cash. However, it taught me two very important lessons. First, it taught me to actually stick to my grocery list and not get sidetracked by that "special finds" aisle at Aldi. Second, it taught me to stick to my budget because of the boundary that cash provided.

Some people might shun credit cards and use a debit card thinking it's similar to using cash. Be careful, though. If your budget is only $100 but you go to check out and the total is $103, you'll likely just swipe your card and move on rather than take an item out. Well, guess what? You're three dollars over your budget. And if you don't adjust your budget, you are going to stay over budget all month long. If you had shopped with just a hundred-dollar bill on you, you'd have been forced to put something back to bring that total down to a hundred dollars. Unlike debit cards, cash provides a practical boundary that helps you stick to your budget.

For me, shopping with cash helped me learn to stay within my grocery budget. Each time I shop, as I pick up an item on my list, I write down its price. Then, right before I head to check out, I tally them all up and factor in the tax. This helps me not only make sure that I have enough cash on me to purchase the groceries, but it also keeps me on budget. If I am over budget,

I can easily find an item to put back, because I recorded the prices of each item right on my grocery list. This method may seem like a lot of work, but it really helps me stay within my budget.

Many of my readers have found that using grocery pickup helps them stick to their budget, since they can see the total as they add items to their online carts. I'm way too much of a control freak to let someone else pick out my produce. But if you have trouble with impulse shopping and the thought of tracking prices makes you want to hyperventilate, then give the online grocery pickup option a try. Remember, living within a budget isn't easy, and it's okay to stumble. But over time, if you keep trying, you will develop habits and methods that will help you succeed.

STEP 8: STAY AWARE

This last step is a little different. In my honest opinion, in the great "How much should you be spending on groceries?" debate, I believe the only way to fully determine that answer is based on you and your family specifically. You need to pay close attention to the food being consumed and not being consumed in your home. You also need to stay aware of how different seasons of your life may impact your budget. If you're in a season when kids are participating in numerous activities, you may not be home often enough to cook every night. This means you may need to come up with either freezer meals or slow cooker meals for those nights, or you may want to lower your grocery budget and up your eating-out budget. Awareness is key in money management. If you aren't aware of what your money is doing, it's not working for you. You work hard for that money, so make sure you manage it well to keep it working for you.

Now maybe, having just read through these steps, you are wondering what in the world your grocery budget has to do with paying off debt and walking the road to financial freedom. Here's the deal, friend: other than debt, nothing eats at your budget more than food. It's true; you know it is. And let's be honest, food prices are always increasing. I just got back from my weekly grocery run, and the price of beef is up 10 percent from just a few months ago. Needless to say, we're going to be eating a lot more chicken for a while.

My point is, if you want to become debt free and achieve your money goals, it's not going to be enough to just rein in your discretionary spending. You're going to need to rein in your grocery spending as well.

What About Beans and Rice?

One of the first questions I get asked when someone hears that we're 100 percent debt free is: "Did you eat a ton of beans and rice?" The short answer is no. We definitely did (and still do) eat recipes that include either or both, but if all we ever ate on our debt-free journey was beans and rice, we would have burned out long before we ever finished the race. Simply put, we like our food. Eating the same thing every single day would just wear us out. But I did learn ways of stretching our meals by using beans and other vegetables. For example, did you know that shredded carrots are actually really tasty in tacos? Frozen veggies tossed with scrambled eggs and rice make an amazing "fried" rice that you can turn into a full meal or have as a side dish. Don't be afraid to get creative in the kitchen. You'll be surprised by how many ways you can stretch meals out without having to eat nothing but beans and rice for days on end.

I do think that the concept of "beans and rice" does get at an important truth, though. When you are working hard to get out of debt or achieve a financial milestone, you need to focus your grocery money on the staples that give you and your family the most nutritional bang for the buck. An easy way to trim your grocery budget is to eliminate snacks, sodas, candy, alcohol, chips, desserts, and so on. I'm not suggesting that you can never have any of these things in your grocery haul. I just want you to be conscious of what your grocery spending is going toward and whether it's serving you and your family well.

Habits Can Change

I know that this was a lot to unpack, and maybe you're feeling a little overwhelmed. But keep in mind, this is a process—a discipline. You're not going to change old habits and build new ones right out of the gate and have them stick. So don't get discouraged or feel like you have too much to do. The biggest thing you need to do is to be aware of what you and your family are currently eating and how much of it you're consuming and throwing away. Then put that knowledge to work for your family. If you only have $150 left after payday for groceries and you've got a family of six to feed, then you're going to need to put that money to work for you.

You've got this. Use the steps outlined in this chapter. Take an inventory of what you already have on hand and make a meal plan and a grocery list. Keep doing this every time you need to go shopping, and before long, you'll have developed the discipline of sticking to your grocery budget!

Let's Make Some Money Moves

1. Review your quick-start budget so you know how much money you have to spend on groceries. Write this amount down on your grocery list to keep it front and center as you shop.
2. Make a list of your family's favorite meals. Assemble the recipes along with a list of the ingredients to help you avoid ordering takeout.
3. Make a weekly meal plan before you head to the store. Take a quick inventory of what you have on hand so you can create a well-thought-out grocery list.
4. Shop for groceries with cash.

Five

TEAMWORK MAKES
THE DREAM WORK

According to a survey by the website MagnifyMoney, 21 percent of divorces are caused by money issues.[1] Honestly, that statistic doesn't surprise me in the least. Money can be a very emotional topic, especially in a marriage. You are two different people with different upbringings, and it's possible that you have competing beliefs around money. We all have feelings toward money—how it should be used and different perspectives on how much is enough. Marital issues with money start after we've made our solemn vows to have and to hold and then discover that our spouse has different opinions about money than we do.

Now, if you are not married and think this chapter doesn't

apply to you, I would still encourage you to read it. I know that Pat and I could have used some of the advice I outline here back when we were dating!

The first thing to bear in mind as a couple is that our childhoods affect how we think about and use money as adults. Think back to your own childhood. How did your parents use money? Did they get their paychecks on Friday and celebrate with shopping sprees only to struggle the rest of the time until the next pay period? Or did you grow up in a super frugal home where you had to wash out the plastic sandwich bags and reuse them? Or did you have a dad who always bought a brand-new truck every two years? Sit for a while and think about being in a store with your parents. How did they spend their money? Did they openly talk about money with you? Did they always seem stressed about money? Was money no big deal when you were growing up? Now compare that with how you handle money. Are there any similarities? Do you avoid all things frugal because you hated how you felt having to wash out all those plastic bags?

I share this exercise to demonstrate that the way you handle money as an adult has been shaped by the way your parents viewed, saved, and spent money. You may choose to handle your money the way your parents did, or you may react against it. Either way, you need to not only come to terms with the way you were raised to handle money but also own up to how you're currently handling your money. It's easy to say, "Oh, he's the saver and I'm the spender." This excuses you from having to work together as a couple to find a happy medium in the way money flows in and out of your home. Also, if you grew up

in poverty, that does not mean you or your family are prede-
termined to fail with money. You can, at any point in your life,
decide to change your family tree.

How to Stop Fighting About Money

Before that fateful spring day in 2013, I don't believe Pat and I
ever had an actual productive conversation about money. Sure,
we fought about money often, but those arguments didn't solve
anything. Maybe you can relate to this. I have found that many
married couples feel the same way. They fight nonstop about
money, but the fights never change anything. Chances are you
and your spouse have been caught up in a dance where one of
you takes the lead and says something the other doesn't like.
This triggers a response that is equally not well received. Before
you know it, you're both doing what you've always done: fighting
without listening. And you're no closer to a positive outcome.

Nothing good ever comes out of fighting. So I want to help
you break out of that cycle. To stop the money fights, I recommend the following simple two-step process.

STEP 1: OWN YOUR OWN FAULTS

Before you talk with your spouse about money, you need to
do some prep work. First, figure out your money mindset and,
in particular, how you use money. It is important that you do
this work before talking to your spouse, because you need to
own how you personally have been handling money. When I

realized just how bad things were, I had to first own up to the mistakes I had made in managing money. I had to look beyond the two-dollar can of Red Bull Pat bought almost every single day. Instead, I had to focus on myself and own up to the fact that I was at fault for our money issues too.

Now, I know no one likes to admit when they're wrong. But I have found that most of the time, big, explosive arguments usually result from one or both parties not accepting responsibility for their part in the issue. It's easy to blame others. Sometimes we get caught up in this loop of looking for how our spouse has done us wrong, forgetting that they are our teammate and not our enemy.

Proverbs 28:13 states: "Whoever conceals their sins does not prosper, but the one who confesses and renounces them finds mercy." I'm a firm believer that when we hold on to the mistakes we've kept hidden, they will creep up on us and seek to destroy us (and our marriages) later on. I want to encourage you to first recognize the ways you've been managing or not managing money. Figure out where you've gone wrong and face up to it.

No shame. No guilt. No matter what you've done, you need to own up to it. It doesn't matter if you've been hiding Amazon packages from your spouse for years. It doesn't matter if you're still paying for that expensive gym membership you never use. It doesn't matter if your need to save more money has resulted in your hiding money from your spouse. It doesn't matter what wrong you've done. All that matters is that you own up to it. Then you'll be prepared for the next step toward stopping your money fights: confession.

Step 2: Confess to Your Spouse

If the thought of confessing your financial shortcomings to your spouse makes your blood run cold, let me stop you right there. You need to let go of the fear that is gripping you. If you married a good person, no matter the current state of your marriage, you need to remind yourself that you and your spouse are teammates, not enemies.

At the end of 2017, I found myself in one of those fear-gripping moments. You would have thought that Pat and I would be way past the need to confess financial faults because, at that moment, we were consumer-debt free, had a fully funded emergency fund, and met monthly for budget meetings. But a big money issue loomed, and to be honest, I was the one behind it.

Truth be told, I never wanted our children to attend public school. So, since we were consumer-debt free and had a hefty savings account, I had decided that our oldest, who was entering kindergarten, should attend a private Christian school. I had prayed about it extensively, and we were given a generous scholarship that made the tuition payments affordable. The school year had started off great, and the school was (and still is) a fantastic school. Our little boy was thriving, and my mama heart couldn't have been prouder. But there was a storm brewing on the horizon—one I was desperately trying to ignore. Even though, yes, we could make the tuition payments, they were still eating up a significant portion of our income. And every little hiccup that happened during this time made paying that tuition harder.

As 2018 approached, I not only needed to reregister our oldest child but had to also register our middle child for kindergarten. I filled out the registration forms and sent in the registration fees and scholarship application. But the cold, hard truth started to seep in: I knew deep in my heart that this was not where God wanted our children. We were already starting to struggle to afford the tuition payment for just one child. I knew, no matter how amazing the school was, trying to send both children there was going to be even harder, if not downright impossible.

"The LORD gave and the LORD has taken away" kept popping up in my mind (Job 1:21). No matter how hard I tried to ignore the stirrings of the Holy Spirit, I couldn't. The financial proof was there in front of me. We simply could not afford to send our two children to this amazing Christian school without going back into debt. I had a choice to make. I could go to my husband and attempt to convince him that we absolutely had to keep sending our boys to this private school and go into debt, or I could let go of my dream of sending the kids to a Christian school.

With tears blurring my vision I confessed the whole thing to Pat. I told him we were already struggling to pay for private school tuition, along with having to pay high self-employment taxes, and we had even taken money from our emergency fund more than once to pay a month's tuition or the quarterly tax. I told him if we kept them enrolled at the school it was more than likely that we'd have to sink ourselves back into debt or wipe out our savings.

After hearing me out, Pat said, "You don't have to cry. We're in this together, and we're going to make it. Look, honey, think about it this way. Driving back and forth to school every day is wearing on you. You're already struggling to keep all the balls you're juggling in the air. Honestly, I think they should go to public school. Not because of the money, but because it makes it difficult for you to be the kind of wife and mom you want to be. You just need to let this go."

Now, before you go thinking that Pat is an incredible unicorn of a husband, let me assure you he's not. Most spouses are just like him. Pat was willing to give me the grace I needed after I confessed how my desire to avoid public school was wreaking financial chaos in our lives.

Think about it. Aren't you a lot nicer to someone who admits they were wrong? Aren't you usually a little more willing to admit where you may have been wrong, too, after they make the first move? I say this because I've found, especially in my marriage, that when one of us goes first and admits they were wrong, the other usually follows suit. Then a real, heartfelt conversation occurs free of animosity, blaming, and guilt trips.

Get on the Same Team

I am going to say possibly the most controversial thing you're ever going to hear come out of anyone's mouth. If you're married, you should absolutely have a joint bank account and view all your money as *ours*, not mine and yours. You're a team, and a team cannot operate effectively unless everyone is on the same playing field.

I fully understand why some couples don't have a joint bank account, but can I give you some food for thought? Pat and I married at twenty-three and twenty-four years old. In many ways we were totally unprepared for life and marriage, and it took us two years before we learned how to handle our money as a couple, instead of as two individuals. Sure, we had a joint checking account, but our money was still very separate, because we never used that account. Instead, we continued to use our own individual accounts we had before we were married. He paid his bills and I paid mine. He was responsible for his truck and credit card payments. I was responsible for my car, credit card, and debt-consolidation loan payments. We even split up how the household bills were to be paid; he paid the rent and any "fun" things like going out to eat with friends, and I paid the other household bills and groceries. We never discussed budget. Sure, I was budgeting my money in my account, but I honestly had no idea what was happening with Pat's account. He, likewise, knew nothing about what was flowing in and out of my account.

You may be thinking that this arrangement was wise because I'm married to a Spender. It made perfect sense for me to protect my hard-earned money. But I believe that by not sharing our money we unintentionally allowed something dark to enter into our marriage. We allowed a level of secrecy to worm its way in, and in my opinion, secrecy can wreck a marriage as easily as adultery. Along with secrecy, I realized that the reason behind our not sharing money had everything to do with fear. I was afraid that he'd spend all the money, and Pat was afraid that I'd never let him spend any of it even when it was needed.

Both of those concerns were (and still are) perfectly valid. But I believe that instead of allowing fear of what could happen to control us, we should allow this fear to be an opportunity to grow closer. Is it possible that this can lead to more fighting? Of course it's possible; but I believe that with the right mindset and focus, we can move from fighting to something productive.

I know this is going to sound so elementary—because it is—but it works. "Teamwork makes the dream work" has become a Fearon family mantra. I truly believe that we tend to forget this in our marriages. We live in a very individualistic society, which isn't altogether bad, but it isn't great either. We work on ourselves and our careers, but we forget to work on our relationships because we're too busy working on ourselves. I've seen this play out numerous times, not only in my own marriage but also in the marriages of others. When we're not working together as a team, the beautiful union that is marriage can start to unravel.

If you want to have a happy and long-lasting relationship with someone, you're going to have to figure out how to be a team player. This was one of the hardest lessons I had to learn in my marriage. I'm selfish by nature. There, I said it. I like what I like. If I want it, I want it; and if I don't want to do it, I don't want to do it.

Goodness, I sound like a two-year-old. But it's true. I'm a naturally selfish person who cares about my interests over my husband's. I don't think I have to tell you just how damaging this mentality is not only to my marriage but to any marriage where unchecked selfishness reigns supreme. Now, please don't confuse my message here. I'm not saying that you shouldn't take care of yourself or that you shouldn't work to improve yourself. You definitely should do those things. Just don't exclude your spouse. Taking care of yourself includes taking care of your spouse. You two are a team, and it's time to start playing on the same field.

Start Talking About Money

So, what does teamwork involving money look like? As we discussed earlier, first, it involves being honest with yourself about how you handle money. Then it involves confessing any flaws you've found. This will begin the healthy process of having open and honest conversations with your spouse about money.

You will then be prepared to talk about other financial issues, such as how to pool your resources, how to cut your spending, or how to save for a down payment on a home. This is also where you can start dreaming together and figuring out a version of the dream life. Having a shared vision for your life together is a powerful unifier. Not only that, but your shared vision will motivate you *individually* to work *together* toward shared goals.

The key to these conversations is remembering that you

two are a team—and a team works together, not against each other. So watch what you say. Don't accuse your spouse of things or pass issues off as *their* problem. Keep in mind that their issues are in fact your issues because you're a team. Make sure to use words like *we*, *us*, and *our*, instead of *me*, *you*, and *I*.

Rather than having a conversation like this:

> You spent thirty dollars on what? I can't believe you would cause us to go over budget for a silly video game! Why do you do this kind of stuff? Can't you see I'm trying to improve us financially and you're destroying that?

have a conversation that sounds more like this:

> We're over budget this month and I'm not sure what we can do to fix it and prevent it from happening again next month. Do you have any ideas how we can work together to fix this? I have a few ideas, but I'd love to hear your thoughts first and figure out a game plan.

The difference between these conversations is that one is accusatory and causes division, whereas the other acknowledges the issue while creating space for problem-solving and unity to happen.

Now, you may look at this example and think, *That's great. It's all rainbows and sunshine. But it would never play out that way in my house.* I totally understand that sentiment because I felt that way for many years. I kept thinking that for changes to happen, I had to be the one to make them happen. In reality, I was forgetting that I wasn't married to myself, and that even though the only person I could control was me, I had to let my husband in and allow him to be a part of the process.

How to Become a Team

What does this whole teamwork thing actually look like in a marriage? Well, it looks like a lot of talking, a lot of listening, and a lot of working out the details together. I know that for many marriages, it takes a lot of work to get to a better place. So I want to offer up some practical advice for getting to that better place. However, please keep in mind that becoming a strongly functioning team will not happen overnight. Depending on the current state of your marriage, this whole process could take a very long time. But don't despair; your marriage is 100 percent worth fighting for.

It took Pat and me about two years before we started reaping the fruit of all our hard work and hard conversations. Please understand, this advice isn't a miracle pill that's going to magically improve your marriage. It is simply meant to show how you can start a beautiful, growing process *together*.

Start by Having Conversations About the Future

I've discovered that it's easier to discuss the stuff in our future than it is to talk about our current money situation.

If you're not used to having hard conversations about money, it may be better to start with the future. Discuss with your spouse all the things they hope to achieve in life, the things the two of you can plan to achieve together. Allow these conversations to usher in your current reality.

For example, if your spouse dreams of being able to own a boat they can take out fishing whenever they want, guilt free, you may want to lead into the conversation like this: "You know, if we paid off the credit cards we could put an extra $200 in savings for that boat. And if we were able to make additional wiggle room in the budget, we'd be able to buy the boat in about two years."

I've discovered that talking about the future allows our minds to open up to new possibilities, because it brings into focus how the direction we are currently moving in may not lead to where we want to end up. That realization can begin many different conversations about how the two of you can achieve the big dreams you both want (your own version of the dream life we talked about in chapter 1). This is why I encourage all married couples to regularly discuss their dreams and desires about the future together.

Divvy Up Your Financial Tasks

Typically, one of you will take greater interest in or have more time or ability to do certain financial tasks. However, even if one person takes on more of the administrative load, the other person should always have input in the decisions about how to handle the money, and they, in turn, should always be respectful and thankful for the administrative work being done.

The way you divvy up your financial tasks should be unique to you and your spouse. Beware of making baseless assumptions, such as "men should be in charge of investing" or "women should be in charge of the household budget." Also, beware of assuming certain tasks or roles belong to one spouse just because that was how your parents did it. Finding the groove that suits you and your spouse may take some time (and maybe some tears), but knowing who's in charge of what task will prevent finger-pointing and help both of you face up to the responsibilities you've worked out. In addition, working together means that no one person is in charge of the family's finances. Just because you do a task does not mean the other person has no say in the matter.

Here are some of the major financial tasks that can be divvied up:

- Create and maintain a budget.
- Plan meals and shop thoughtfully for groceries.
- File taxes.
- Pay bills.
- Research ways to cut spending.
- Research vacation options within your budget.
- Research and purchase life, health, auto, home, and/or disability insurance.
- Decide on Christmas/birthday budget and shop for gifts.

- Research and maintain retirement investments.
- Decide on major expenditures, such as buying a new appliance or an HVAC system, research how much they will cost, and implement how to pay for them.

If there is a certain task you both dislike, such as filing taxes, either agree to take turns dealing with it or reward the entrusted spouse with something they enjoy when the task is done.

In our marriage I'm the saver, so I've taken on the chore of creating and maintaining our budget (with Pat's input, of course), including a special interest in cutting our expenses, especially our grocery budget. Because I work from home and have the time and interest, I also pay bills, file personal income taxes, and invest our money for retirement. Meanwhile, Pat is the spender, so he takes on the chore of researching our major expenditures (reporting back to me, of course). And since he runs his own business, he handles all the budgeting, bookkeeping, and taxes associated with that—except expenses that affect our family budget, such as our quarterly estimated income taxes, which we discuss together. We both like to shop for Christmas presents, so that is a task we share.

Even if you are not in charge of a certain financial task, you should still have a cursory understanding of what it entails, along with a healthy respect for the time, effort, and emotional burden required to handle it. If your spouse is doing a great job cutting grocery expenses, be sure to thank them. If you've set up a retirement account, make sure your spouse knows how to access it in case something happens to you, and be sure to share with your spouse the burden of making investment decisions.

Which brings me to my next point.

Schedule Regular Money Check-Ins with Your Spouse

The other practice that is super important to the financial health of your marriage is to have regular money check-ins with your spouse. Normally this would be once a month, but you can meet more frequently if you both feel it's necessary, like we did when we first began our debt-free journey, or if something important comes up that needs to be discussed right away. This doesn't have to be a formal meeting, but it helps to schedule the meeting on the calendar so it doesn't get lost in the shuffle.

Prepare any necessary documents to bring to the meeting, such as a copy of your quick-start budget or your report on what it will cost to replace your roof. You might also want to bring a list of issues you need to discuss, such as how to pay upcoming taxes, whether to replace your furnace now or later, or who should research potential Realtors for your upcoming home search.

Here's how our typical monthly money meeting goes. I bring our budget binder and my laptop to the dining room table along with a notebook and pen. Then Pat and I discuss any issues that popped up the previous month. If we went over budget in a certain area, we identify the reason why and how we can prevent it from happening again. We also discuss if that budget category needs to be upped, such as the grocery budget because the price of certain produce went up. From there, we discuss how we're doing with our savings and where we are currently in regard to meeting certain goals. Then we discuss all our future plans. Pat is always looking for opportunities to spend money. If his current want is to put sod in the front yard, that's the future item that's up for discussion. We'll discuss how much money we need to set aside, if we are achieving our savings goal, and anything else we need to put in motion for that goal to happen.

That's the extent of our meetings today. But when we were deep in debt and trying to figure out this whole teamwork style of managing money, we met once a week. This weekly meeting went on for years until we finally established a rhythm that worked for us. Then we were able to scale back the meetings to once a month.

Sometimes Pat and I even have our financial meetings over the phone instead of in person. I mention this because if you're married to someone who travels a lot for work, don't be reluctant to have these conversations over the phone or Skype. These meetings don't have to look a certain way; they just have to produce positive results.

SET A SPENDING-LIMIT THRESHOLD

Having a spending-limit threshold is super important, and it will help protect and enhance the trust between you and your spouse.

This limit for Pat and me has changed over the years as our finances have changed. Essentially, we don't make large purchases over a specific amount without the other's approval. Let's say, for example, that Pat wants to buy a new table saw that's $600. He would need to discuss it with me before making the purchase, and we'd have to decide together if this is an immediate need or if we have time to set up a sinking fund to build up the money to pay for it. Now let's say Pat breaks the phone holder he has in his truck to hold his phone while driving. That purchase is only twenty dollars, and he's free to spend the money without first consulting me. Yes, he'll have to let me know that he spent twenty dollars that wasn't originally planned so I can adjust our budget, but he doesn't need my agreement beforehand.

This spending-limit threshold has worked well in our family as a way to allow Pat the freedom to spend money guilt free within boundaries as well as give us a specific cue when we need to have a more in-depth conversation. This spending limit is also helpful if you have someone who is consistently asking you for money and you feel bad telling them no. You can now tell them, "I'll need to discuss lending you $100 with my husband before I can give it to you. We have a family rule that we always agree on spending money that is over $100 before we do it." This is a great way to protect your family's finances, and it helps to make sure that you are working as a team and making good decisions that aren't influenced by fatigue, guilt, emotions, or pressure (external or internal).

It may take a while to get the hang of working together as

a team, especially if you're used to fighting with your spouse about money. But I believe, with practice, you and your spouse are going to reap tremendous rewards. Remember, you are a team, and teamwork makes the dream work!

Let's Make Some Money Moves

1. Identify any areas where you may need to come clean to your spouse regarding your family's finances. Confess those problem areas to your spouse.
2. Have an open and honest conversation with your spouse about your future. Discuss how proper money management can help you get closer to achieving your goals.
3. Divvy up your financial tasks, such as making and maintaining a budget, filing taxes, and so on.
4. Set up regularly occurring money meetings to discuss where you are financially and make necessary adjustments.

Six

AFFORDING CHILDREN

Recently, I saw a Facebook post from someone wondering, "Why do broke people have children?" He even shared a whole slew of awful opinions on why you shouldn't have children unless you make over six figures a year!

This guy is hardly the only one to share this particular sentiment. I've heard it many times both online and in real life. I remember a trip to Aldi with my two young children while pregnant with my third. As I unloaded the kids from my husband's thirteen-year-old pickup truck with its tailgate held together with Bondo, the middle-aged woman loading her groceries next to me asked, "Don't you know they make a thing called birth control that would help you get on your feet?"

No, I'm not kidding. And I've never forgotten it, because my three-year-old then asked me, "Mommy, what's burf control?"

There are a lot of misconceptions when it comes to having children and affording their care. Are there major expenses that can completely crush a family financially? Absolutely. But, outside of day care and major medical needs, most other expenses pertaining to children don't have to be high. There are ways to lower expenses like clothing and groceries. As a parent you get to decide what you will and will not pay for. You get to decide if you will buy your kids a tablet or cell phone, or if that is something you will expect your children to save for and purchase themselves. The same goes for other expenses like their first car, sports, college, and even their weddings. You are the parents of your children and you get to decide.

Many people believe you need to provide the very best you can for your children. But the definition of "the very best" can differ dramatically. For some parents that means giving their children everything they never had growing up. For others, it means making them earn all those things so they learn the value of money. There are about a million and one opinions for how to be a good parent. The opinions surrounding what a parent should do in terms of money spent on their children are endless. And honestly, I don't think any of them are perfect.

We have three children, and each one has come with their own set of expenses. The health insurance we carried at the time that each child was born determined just how much it cost to bring them home from the hospital. The interests and abilities of our children have determined the cost of their extracurricular activities. Even our schooling choices have costs associated with them. There are a lot of variables involved when raising children, and frankly, children aren't meant to be a line item on a balance sheet. But since the cost of raising children is something I'm asked about often, let's talk about what it realistically looks like to raise a family and still achieve your money goals.

Being Intentional Matters

No matter what your parenting philosophy is, it's important that you're intentional. This means creating your family life out of your own intentional choices instead of allowing your family background, peer pressure, or culture to dictate how you raise your kids. Remember our discussion about the dream life? Being intentional means keeping *your* version of the dream life front and center so you will always make choices that allow you to achieve that dream.

When we became pregnant in 2011 with our first child, we were right in the middle of purchasing our home. Pat was a self-employed sole proprietor, and I was an administrative project manager with an engineering company in Atlanta. We quickly realized that once our baby arrived, our income would change dramatically. As you may recall, Pat and I had already made the decision that I would be a stay-at-home mom. This made a difference in the amount of money we would have available for our family moving forward.

Living intentionally requires that you take action toward the life you want to build. Honestly, I was nervous about quitting my job. I had been working since high school, and the thought of not having a job was odd. Also, I panicked at the thought of relying on someone else financially. For my own peace of mind, I had to figure out if we actually could do this.

Shortly after we signed on the dotted line for our mortgage, I called my HR department and asked them to change my direct deposit from our checking account to our savings account. In the seven months before our baby was born, I intended to learn how to live off my husband's income while we saved mine.

The first few months of living on Pat's income alone were tough. Not only did Pat and I not communicate well about money, but we had grown very accustomed to the lifestyle that having two incomes had given us. We were also still stuck in the trap of "your money" versus "my money" instead of the "our money" school of thought. But over time, we slowly got better at living off Pat's income while simultaneously building up our savings account.

On January 11, 2012, with the birth of our first child, I officially became a stay-at-home mom. It was a very scary leap. But it was made less scary by the fact that we had practiced living this way for months. Before we began this experiment, our savings had a little more than a hundred dollars. By keeping our eyes fixed on the goal of my being a stay-at-home mom, we had roughly $5,000 saved to act as a cushion when we began living our new lifestyle. We were being intentional about the life we were trying to build so we wouldn't be caught up in a lifestyle we didn't want.

Having Choices

Before I move on, I need to address the elephant in the room. In the past, it was not only perfectly acceptable for a mom to stay home with her children but our culture expected it! Now, however, our society has shifted in the opposite direction. Many people believe that a woman should never stay home with her children and should instead keep advancing in her career. But if we believe that women should be able to have choices about how to live their own lives, then we need to stop trying to decide for them what their lives should look like.

I share this because I do not believe that anyone, mother or father, should be required to stay home and care for their children. I believe families should have the choice to live however they feel is best without being judged by society.

We nearly lost out on living our dream due to our over-spending, paycheck-to-paycheck lifestyle and our overall lack of proper money management. These things made us realize that our goal of my staying home with our children was on the line. The thought of missing out on our goal is what motivated us to take charge of our financial lives.

Again, I am certainly not telling you that you or your spouse must stay home with your children. But I do believe that a part of having financial freedom is having options. After all, what kinds of options would you have if you didn't require two incomes to survive? Living with intention means that you evaluate where your current lifestyle is taking you and, if needed, make the necessary changes to reach your goal.

The Two-Income Trap

Have you ever noticed that whenever you or your spouse gets a pay raise it feels amazing, but within a few months, it starts to feel like you're back to not making enough money again? Your paycheck gets bigger, but without intention and proper boundaries in place, you end up spending the additional money without realizing it.

This phenomenon is called the two-income trap, and it can make it seem impossible for one of the income earners to stop working. It's worse if one of the income earners loses their job unexpectedly. Sadly, many families fall into bankruptcy when this happens.

This two-income trap keeps many middle-class families stuck. They can't move up, and moving down seems impossible. These households are usually not aware of how "stuck" they really are until they try to get out of it. Many times, when they're living paycheck to paycheck, they get caught in this trap of never having enough income to make their life work. And it comes as no surprise that most of these families are also deep in the trenches of parenting and trying to provide a quality family life for their children.

The only way to escape the two-income trap is to intentionally design your family budget around one income. The other income then becomes bonus money instead of essential money. This way of living allows a level of financial freedom so if the one income suddenly disappeared, your family would still be okay. The bonus income would take over and your household would only experience a hiccup versus a full-fledged financial catastrophe. Remember, it doesn't matter how much money you make. What matters is how you spend it.

When the Great Recession hit in 2008, Pat and I were newly engaged, and I was still working for the engineering company in Atlanta. Honestly, I was already too broke to notice a recession. But I was very aware of what was happening to those around me.

I had a wonderful coworker, the mother of four beautiful children who was married to a hard-working blue-collar man. I will never forget the day I walked into the ladies' restroom and caught her sobbing. Her husband had lost everything. His business was gone and he was struggling to find employment, and since she didn't make enough money to support their family on her own, they were now losing their home. She was terrified not only for herself but also for her four children. Where were they going to live? Even the Econo Lodge down the road was too expensive for them! They were deep in over their heads, and the pain my coworker felt was crushing.

Many of you have experienced financial trauma, whether it was a result of the Great Recession, the COVID-19 pandemic, or other life circumstances. You may know the fear and pain of losing your sense of safety and security. If you are a dual-income household, one of the best ways to regain that security is to get intentional about living on one income. Design your life in such a way that your family could survive even if one of you lost your job, lost your life, or even just decided to stay home with the kids.

Does this mean you have to drastically upend the life you're currently living with two incomes? Not necessarily. The biggest point here is to get focused. Most of us aren't actively paying attention to the flow of money in and out of our homes. We pay for Little League, dance, gymnastics, softball. We pay the minimum on all our debts and attempt to make everything work. But a lot of the time, everything would end up working if we purposefully designed it to, if we just sat down and got intentional on where the money is coming in and where it is going out.

How to Pay for All Those Extras

As a child, I wasn't allowed to participate in sports or extracurricular activities. If I'm honest, it made me really sad. But now, as a mom to three kids, I can attest to just how ridiculously expensive kids' sports and extracurricular activities are! I now completely understand why my mom said no to those things.

Just like my mom, you get to decide how many extracurriculars your children are going to be a part of, if any. You also get to decide the budget for those activities and how much you're willing to spend. Being intentional and designing your family's life around your budget involves every area, including the extracurriculars that take the family outside the home.

I can't tell you what rules to implement when it comes to your kids' lives. But I can tell you the Fearon household rules, and maybe they will help you if you're struggling with navigating the world of kids' expenses. We allow our kids one extracurricular per season. Which means that if one of my boys wants to play both soccer and football in the fall, he'll have to choose the one he wants to do more because he can't do both without it causing chaos. We also have a strict rule that there will be no extracurricular activities on Sunday.

As far as money goes, we will pay for registration dues and basic uniforms. However, if our children want special items beyond the basic requirements, then they are required to use their money to pay for them. This not only keeps the expenses down, but it teaches our kids that things like the designer version of their uniform come at a premium. It also helps them learn to make decisions and accept the outcomes of those decisions. Another benefit is that it helps them see things a bit differently when they are the ones footing the bill.

While our family's extracurricular activities tend to focus on sports, don't forget the costs of other interests, such as music lessons, drama, chess club, robotics, or individual hobbies like horseback riding. One great way to save money is to figure out your kids' interests and capabilities. If your son shows no interest in piano and your daughter hates going to dance class, why invest in that? Pat and I like to think about what our children will be like when they are thirty years old. Since each of them is unique, this helps us to find ways to guide them in the way God made them, and it helps us be much more intentional in our parenting. And let's not forget that an extracurricular activity can be a job or a business endeavor. Encouraging your children to get creative and come up with various ways to earn money on their own can be a great method of intentionally helping them develop those entrepreneurial skills!

Frankly, a lot of parents get caught up in the extracurricular race because "everyone is doing it" or they think their child won't get into a good college without a long list of activities. The cost of college alone is enough to scare a lot of parents. But you can be intentional about that cost too.

Saving for Your Children's Future

The hope of most parents is not only to provide for their children as they are growing up but also to successfully launch them into their adult life. And many parents assume that a successful launch includes paying for their college expenses. So you may be shocked to hear that Pat and I are not specifically saving for our children's college educations.

Hear me out.

When Pat and I first discussed saving money for college, I was the one who was all gung ho on the idea. Pat, on the other hand, had zero interest. We did end up finding common ground. But before we found it, we had to have an intentional discussion about how much and in what ways we would support our children financially as they launched into adulthood.

Now, maybe this will make me sound like a horrible mom, but I don't believe college is the be-all and end-all to a happy and successful life. I'm a college graduate. In fact, we've been discussing my going back to college for my master's degree. Trust me, my family values college education. I wouldn't be where I am today without it, so I completely understand how valuable college can be. But I also know that college isn't for everyone, nor does it guarantee a rewarding career. Many people today have big, fancy, expensive college degrees and are making less money per year than what their degrees cost them.

I truly believe we have been sold a bill of goods with the idea that the only way to ever make it in life is to have a college degree. Of course, some professions require a college degree, like becoming a teacher, a doctor, or a lawyer. But it's dangerous to fall into the belief that without a college degree you can't start a business, build a career you love, or be financially successful.

That's not a belief I plan to pass down to my children. I don't want my children penalized for not going to college when they attempt to access money that Pat and I saved for them. That is why we do not invest in 529 plans. I don't have anything against 529 accounts; they are great investment vehicles if you plan to pay for your children's college education. But if you have doubts about whether college will be right for your children, you might want to try our idea.

Instead of saving for college, Pat and I have what we call

"life accounts" for each of our three children. These accounts are high-yield savings accounts. They do not earn as much as a 529 would, but our children will not be penalized if they decide not to attend college. They can use this money to help pay for college, their wedding, a down payment on a home, or even start a business. And since Mom and Dad already paid the tax on the money, they won't have to worry about it. Whatever is in those accounts belongs to them, and hopefully, by the grace of God, we will have done our job and trained up our children in proper money management so it will be put to good use.

How do these life accounts work? We contribute money to these accounts on every birthday, holiday, and special occasion, such as a graduation. We also asked our children's grand-parents, godparents, and extended family to consider giving to their life accounts in lieu of physical gifts.

The big picture, though, is that you should not feel obliged to save for your children's futures at all. In fact, if you can save for only one big future expense, it should be for your own retirement, not for college to launch your child. Plenty of kids who were launched out on their own at age eighteen without parental help still made a good life for themselves (this includes both me and my husband).

Don't feel guilty if you decide that all your family can afford is the basics in food, shelter, and clothing. Nowhere in a "how to raise children" rule book does it state that in order to be a good parent you must provide your children with every luxury and every opportunity.

What matters, again, is that you are intentional. Talk with

your spouse about how you plan to launch your children, and when your children are able to think about their future, talk to them too. Let them know what to expect from you in the years ahead in terms of practical and financial help as they enter adulthood. This will give them a vision for their own future and help them to be intentional in their choices. If your child really wants to attend college but they know you will not be paying its full cost, they may be motivated to get good grades, save money from part-time jobs, apply for scholarships, or enlist in the military to help pay the balance. A little self-reliance never hurt anyone.

Saving for College

If you decide that saving for college is a priority for your family, you have two major options: a 529 plan or an education savings account (ESA). They are similar in almost every way except that the ESA has an annual contribution limit of only $2,000, while the 529 allows you to contribute up to $15,000 or even more. For that reason alone, most people save for college using a 529 plan.

Typically, you will enroll for a 529 through your state. You can buy into another state's plan, but your own state's 529 might come with some advantages, such as a tax break on your state income tax. So when you research 529 plans, start with your own state first. If your state gets generally high ratings for low fees and high performance, it's probably best to use it. But if it's rated low because it charges high fees or its investments don't perform well, you may want to choose one from another state.

A 529 plan is an investment account, which means that the money is generally invested in stocks and bonds, and it is intended to grow over the long term (longer than five years). This money isn't going to be liquid like a regular savings account at your bank. However, the growth will be both tax and penalty free as long as the funds are used for higher education expenses.

When you have a 529 plan, you will need to choose how to invest the money. Typically, if college is more than ten years away, your investments will be heavier in stocks. As college nears, your investments will shift to safer, less volatile investments, such as bonds or even money markets.

These plans are great for saving for college because they are available to you regardless of your income level, and you can use the funds to pay for all college-related expenses, including application fees, dorm rooms, and books. However, if you use the money for anything else, you will be hit with a federal tax and a penalty of 10 percent. If one of your children decides not to attend college, you can move their 529 money into another child's account, which provides for some flexibility.

Bear in mind that these accounts are not just for the traditional academic version of four-year colleges and universities. They can also be used for community colleges and trade schools. So you can steer your kids in the direction of their aptitudes and interests, from beauty school to the culinary arts to trades such as plumbing, HVAC, welding, auto repair, electrical work, and carpentry.

What Really Matters

After reading this chapter, you might have that weird, anxious feeling that you're not doing enough for your kids. Remember, the only thing that truly matters to your child is the loving presence you give them. My parents didn't have the money to pay for my college education, nor did they have the money to pay for my wedding. My in-laws also didn't have the money to pay either for their boys. And you know what? We turned out all right.

Beyond their basic needs, your kids don't need your money. But they do need your presence, love, support, and discipline to help mold them into the amazing men and women they will grow up to be. Don't allow the world to tell you what is right for your family. You know best.

Let's Make Some Money Moves

1. Live intentionally. If you plan to have children, what do you want your life to look like as a family? If you already have children, is your current lifestyle sustainable financially and emotionally?

2. If you are a dual-income couple, is there a way to tailor your lifestyle to fit just one income in case either of you were to lose your job? If so, make a plan for that second income. For example, you might want to pay off debt, open an emergency fund, or save up for a down payment on a house.

3. Discuss with your spouse what, as parents, you're willing to pay for and what you believe should be your children's responsibility.

4. Decide whether to save for your children's college education or set up a life account or both. Then research 529 plans if you are planning on college, or high-interest savings accounts if you are planning on a life account. Determine how much money you can put into those accounts each month or year.

Seven

CRISIS MODE

Have you ever had a moment that completely wrecked you? For us, that moment came when Pat fell out of a two-story window while at work. I will never forget that phone call as long as I live. I've also never been more grateful to God. Even though the fall was brutal and resulted in Pat shattering his right elbow and left wrist, he was alive. But we didn't realize that a financial storm that had been brewing on the horizon was now fast approaching.

After I had taken Pat to the hospital, where they X-rayed and bandaged him with instructions to follow up with the orthopedic surgeon and schedule surgery, the intake nurse informed us that Pat's employer didn't have workers' compensation insurance. We gave her our health insurance information, but she warned us that it might get rejected because it was a work-related injury.

And sure enough, the claim was denied. That left us with not only the emergency room bill but also the responsibility of having to pay for the surgery Pat desperately needed in the morning. He was in danger of losing mobility in his dominant hand if surgery wasn't performed quickly. We had one of two options: find a credit card with a limit high enough to pay for both the ER and the surgery or completely drain our savings account.

There wasn't enough time to apply for a credit card since the surgery needed to happen within twenty-four hours to prevent further nerve damage. Consequently, I transferred—to the exact penny—the full amount of our savings account into our checking account. I cried as I stood in front of the admission office as the woman behind the counter told me, "Honey, if you don't pay right now they will not take him into surgery. You can fight with his boss later about the money, but he won't be seen without payment in full. Hospital policy."

Writing that check was one of the hardest things I've ever had to do. I'm someone who feels safe and secure with a beefy savings account. The very fact that I, a mom to a not even one-year-old with a baby on the way, was going to have to live without this safety net scared me more than I could ever put into words.

At this point, we were not only Floaters but also Daredevils—living without a savings account. In addition, Pat couldn't work for several weeks after his surgery, but we still had bills to pay. I was a stay-at-home mom, and there was no way Pat could chase after a rambunctious one-year-old while he was healing. So in a moment of sheer desperation, I started walking dogs for extra money. During this time of uncertainty, I also started my first blog *The Budget Mama*.

Honestly, I had no idea what I was going to blog about. Here I was, a woman with a degree from one of the top accounting schools in the Southeast yet failing to manage my own family's finances. It didn't make sense to me. I mean, how could we be failing? I had the intellect and all the right credentials, and I knew in my heart that Pat's income was enough. So how did we get here?

The answer includes a multitude of reasons, but we're going to start with the one in front of us. We may have gone into this scary moment with a savings account, but we had no real *savings plan* in place. We had no strategy for the future. We didn't know if the money we had saved was enough. We simply had money in a savings account because that's what we were supposed to do. We had no idea as to why we needed a savings account, the amount we needed to have in it, or how to maintain it.

What Is an Emergency Fund?

By now you've certainly heard the term *emergency fund*. It's a cute little name given to a savings account that's supposed to be designated for emergencies only. You may also have heard that you should start with only $1,000. I don't exactly agree with this advice. That emergency surgery my husband had to have? The grand total was over $3,000! That completely wiped out our savings—and we thought we were doing well financially back then because we were the only young couple we knew who actually had a savings account.

I understand why $1,000 is given as the starting target for your emergency fund. Many people don't even have that in their savings account. But I believe the dollar amount should be something that reflects your actual life. For example, if you have children, $1,000 could easily be wiped out with a broken bone or wrecked car. This is why I encourage you to think carefully about how large your starter emergency fund needs to be, then save up accordingly.

The only way to no longer live as a Daredevil is to make sure you have a savings account that can survive the ups and downs of your life. It does you no good if your emergency fund cannot cover an emergency.

What Is an Emergency?

Let's look at the purpose of an emergency fund. It's not a vacation fund or a Christmas fund. It is a fund that is meant to protect you and your family when life gets turned upside down. It is meant to be a safety net while you work to stabilize your financial lives.

I know some of these things are not fun to think about, but

we must think about them and prepare for them. What happens if your spouse loses their job unexpectedly? Could you afford to survive for a few months with zero income? Would you still be going out to lunch dates and buying everything your favorite influencers on Instagram say you need? No, of course not. Because then your family's life would be turned completely on its head! You would be in survival mode during that time.

This is when the emergency fund kicks into gear. It gets used in actual dire emergencies. Does that mean this account can be used only if you or your spouse loses your job or one of you loses your life? No. There are other emergencies that may require you to dip into the emergency fund. Let's say it is a 90-degree day and your HVAC dies. Yep, down here in the South that would qualify as an emergency. However, a routine car repair, new furniture, or a vacation does not.

You cannot look at your emergency fund as "free money" or something to dip into every time you have unexpected expenses. Its sole purpose is to keep your family afloat when life gets hard. That's why I disagree with the advice of having only $1,000 saved, and instead encourage you to build up an emergency fund that can sustain your family for at least six months with no income.

Building Your Starter Emergency Fund

In chapter 12 we will revisit the topic of building a true, fully funded, six-month emergency fund. But for now, let's look at the steps for creating what I call a "starter" emergency fund, one that provides a small cushion while also getting you into the savings habit.

STEP 1: DETERMINE YOUR ESSENTIAL MONTHLY EXPENSES, THEN MULTIPLY BY SIX

Figure out how much money you will need in your emergency fund. To do this, you're going to start with the end in mind—that is, your family's expenses at the end of six months.

You'll need to go through all your essential monthly expenses, add them up, and then multiply it by six. Essential expenses include, but are not limited to, groceries (not eating out), fuel or other transportation-related costs, rent or mortgage payments, utility and insurance payments, medical expenses, debt payments, and any other essential expenses unique to your family. By "essential" I mean what you need to live, not the fun stuff or the stuff you want to have and like to do. We're talking about the stuff that without it you and your family would not be able to survive. If you're having trouble knowing which expenses to include, a good question to ask yourself is: What expenses would we need to keep paying even if we lost all of our income?

I warn you, though, that amount will likely be pretty large. Maybe over $10,000 or even over $20,000. Don't freak out when you see a high number. It's your ending point, not where you're starting. We're simply getting the ball rolling with this exercise.

STEP 2: PICK A STARTING POINT FOR
YOUR SAVINGS GOAL

Pick your starting point for your starter emergency fund. If $20,000 is what you would need to survive for six months without an income (what I'll call your "fully funded emergency fund"), don't choose $20,000 as your initial savings goal. If you do, you might get overwhelmed and abandon the whole idea. Instead, pick a smaller but very doable starting point.

Your starting point should be an amount that you could save fairly easily within the next three months. I personally like the idea of starting at $3,000, but depending on your own personal situation, you may choose to start at $2,000 or $5,000. However, if you find that saving only $1,000 is the most realistic for you and your family, there's no shame in that. You'll still have more in savings than most people! Again, the point of this process is not to overwhelm you but to get you excited about watching your savings grow and building up this starter emergency fund as quickly as possible.

STEP 3: REVIEW YOUR BUDGET AND
SET ASIDE MONEY TO SAVE

Budget for this starter emergency fund. Review your quick-start budget and determine how much you can afford to set aside. Please don't fret if the amount is small. Five dollars is still more than zero dollars. Every little bit helps. Don't discredit small amounts. But do make a plan to start actively putting that money into the fund.

Now, before I jump into ways to help find some extra

money so you can quickly beef up your starter emergency fund, I recommend that you set up an account with a bank that offers a high-yield savings account. You may need to first save the money in a different account to get to the required minimum opening balance, but I highly encourage you to use these accounts. They are an easy way to earn more money on top of the money you're already saving.

We use internet banks for all our savings accounts because they offer no fees and higher APYs (annual percentage yields) than your traditional brick-and-mortar bank. This also allows for that money to be somewhat of an "out of sight, out of mind" type of deal. If you or your spouse struggles with overspending, having a separate account for your emergency fund can be a great way to make sure the money is not always in front of you when you pay your bills online.

Finding Extra Money

I know saving money can seem impossible. In 2013, Pat and I started with zero in savings (due to Pat's fall out the window), and we were deep in debt. We were terrified, and the idea of saving any kind of money when we were already stretched so thin seemed, well, a little ridiculous. But we soon discovered that the only thing standing in the way of our being able to save money was us. Once we started getting creative, we found that there are actually a lot of ways you can make saving money a reality.

One of the quickest ways we found to add additional cash to our savings account was to sell anything and everything in our home that we didn't need. Most of us have at least one closet full of stuff we never use—or maybe even an entire garage full. Believe it or not, people will pay for a lot of that stuff. Now, don't get me wrong, people are not going to pay full price for something that's been used or has been sitting around your home collecting dust. But they will pay you something. Don't get caught up in thinking, *It cost me $100 brand new, so there's no way I can sell it for only $40.* Because the truth is, that money is already gone. You already spent that money on that item. You can either not recoup a single dime from it and let it continue to sit and collect dust or earn something from it—something that can get you so much closer to achieving your financial goals.

You can also find extra money by putting your bonuses and tax refunds directly into your emergency fund. Trust me, if you don't immediately put that money to work for your future self, it will slip right through your fingers and be gone. Before it can grow legs and walk out of your life, put that bonus money to work and save it.

Another way to find additional money is to look over your calendar and find one morning or afternoon when you have a little bit of free time. Then schedule one hour to make phone calls to your various utility and insurance providers to do some research on new rates. You'll be surprised how quickly these seemingly small amounts of money add up. We recently did this with our natural gas company. I'm a little embarrassed to admit this because I had not been paying attention to how much of an increase our per therm rate had gone up. (A therm is a unit of measurement for your natural gas usage.) We were paying over $2 per therm. No wonder the winter months' budget was getting tight! I called a few other providers and switched to another company with a rate of $0.32 per therm! This process took me maybe fifteen minutes, and we saved $1.68 per therm on our gas bill. We ended up using 40 therms the following winter, so we saved over $60 on just one bill!

Now, if you were to do this with all your bills, you could be adding some serious cash to your starter emergency fund! But the key here is to actually move that savings into your emergency fund. Meaning, once you've made this additional room in your budget, you need to actually put that amount into the emergency fund. Don't fall into the trap of allowing that extra money to just remain something written on paper. It needs to be moved to your emergency fund in order to benefit your future self.

One of the last ways we found extra money was to add additional streams of income. Shortly after our revelation about how badly things were going for our family, I started walking dogs in a townhome community not too far from our home. That meant I was not only walking five or more dogs on a given afternoon, but I was also picking up their poop. To this day, Pat loves to tell people how proud he was of me for being willing to do what had to be done for our family.

I walked dogs while pregnant and chasing my toddler in the Georgia heat! I share this because I absolutely hated that job. Some of the dogs were wonderful and I loved them. But others were not so great and had to be walked separately. I would have to walk dogs in batches, which took up a large part of my afternoon, and, of course, it's always hotter in the middle of the day than in the morning. There were days when every part of me wanted to give up. I didn't want to load up my fussy kids who hated their car seats and drive the half mile to that little townhome community to walk all those dogs and pick up all that poop. But I did. I showed up and went to work.

The Proverbs 31 woman gets talked about a lot in Christian circles. In fact, sometimes that woman can intimidate us moms just trying to keep our heads above the water. But I don't believe she was some mystical do-it-all Wonder Woman. Instead, I think she was a woman who was not afraid to do what needed to be done for her family. Proverbs 31:18 says: "She sees that her trading is profitable, and her lamp does not go out at night." I don't believe this means she never sleeps. Instead, I think it means that her family has the money to pay for the oil to keep that lamp lit all night long, and she contributes to her family's income. Now, I'm not a theologian, so maybe I'm completely wrong here. But I do believe that when we are willing to do what it takes for our families, we will reap the reward of that labor.

It doesn't matter if it's a side hustle, a second job, selling off your used belongings, or simply no longer spending money on things you don't actually need. Your version of contributing to your family's financial health will not look the same as your neighbor's. Just don't be afraid to do what needs to be done to propel your family toward the life and dreams you desire to achieve.

Hustle Culture?

Before I move on, I want to address something that has sprung up over the last few years called the hustle culture—the idea that in an effort to be more and do more, you have to hustle and hustle hard. It tells you not to allow anything or anyone to stand in the way of achieving your dreams, to put blinders on so you won't get distracted by life, and to stay the course of working toward achieving your dreams. The reality is, though, it often leads to losing things that are more precious than the goals you're trying to achieve. You end up losing relationships or your physical or mental health, all in the name of achieving more.

I know you could read that last section about me walking the dogs and think I'm attempting to sell you more of that toxicity. Please trust that I am not. I do not want to suggest that you should fall prey to the lure of the hustle culture. But I do believe in seasons of hustle. Hustle, in and of itself, is not a bad thing. It becomes a bad thing only when it becomes an addiction or an idol rather than a means to help your family move past your current circumstances. I am certainly not trying to convince you to never spend time with your family or to destroy your life by hustling for financial gain.

What I want is for you to hustle when you're in that season

of life when your family needs you. Hustle for about three months to build up that starter emergency fund, then take a break. Take your family on an epic camping trip. Pause the hustle and allow yourself to breathe. Hustle is meant to be a season, and yes, it's a season you'll see many times over the course of your life. You'll see it when you decide to go back to school and finish that degree. You'll see it when you decide to adopt a child. You'll see it when you decide to start your own business or when you change careers. You'll see it when any major life change happens. And that's okay, because hustle is only a season. Don't be afraid to do what you need to do in that season. Remember, hustle is not a bad thing, but don't allow it to overtake your life.

Emergencies *Will* Happen

Here's a little something to keep in mind, even if it might seem glaringly obvious: at some point in your life, you are going to use your emergency fund. For all my fellow savers out there, hear me loud and clear: just because you find yourself in dire need of using your emergency fund, it does not mean you're starting over. It does not mean you've failed. In fact, you have actually succeeded. Because of your prudent planning, you've avoided having to sink back into debt. You've used the emergency fund for an emergency, and that is what it's for.

Right before our lives were turned upside down by the COVID-19 pandemic, our middle child broke his arm in a bike accident. It was a bad break and required surgery. At the end of the day, the bills for this bike accident totaled nearly $12,000! The hospital was willing to give us a generous discount of 50 percent on the bills if we paid in full within thirty days. Since we do not have traditional health insurance and instead use a health-care sharing ministry, we knew we'd be reimbursed on the bills, but we weren't sure when, especially due to the pandemic and potential lag times in processing. So we paid up front for these bills.

If this accident had happened six years ago, we would not have had even half of what we needed to pay up front in our emergency fund. The mere thought of paying nearly $6,000 outright would not have even been on our radar all those years ago. Did I like making that transfer from savings to checking and handing over that hard-earned money the second time? No, definitely not. But you know what it allowed us to do? We were able to survive a broken bone, a historic pandemic, and an economic crisis, because not only did we have a fully funded emergency fund, but we also had no other debts to stress over.

Since we're on the subject of the great pandemic, let me say that I know that a lot of families fell on extremely hard times during the shutdowns and quarantines. Those hard times illustrate why an emergency fund is so very vital to your family's well-being. To me, having a starter emergency fund is more important than rapid-fire paying off debt. (We will talk more about the importance of maintaining a *fully funded* emergency fund of six months in chapter 12.) I don't take lightly the fact that my family, financially speaking, wasn't harmed by the pandemic. I know we were blessed, and I also know, without a shadow of a doubt, that if the pandemic had happened seven years ago, my family would have been devastated financially.

I won't pretend to know what the pandemic was like for you financially, but I do want to encourage you to give yourself and your family the gift of never having to live through something like that again. Did Pat and I know some virus was going to take over the world, causing the economy to come to a grinding halt? No, of course not. But we did know that something—anything—would happen at some point. Being a stay-at-home mom, I knew that something horrible could happen to Pat and I could find myself trying to raise three little kids alone. I could be facing that tragic new reality either with whatever amount is sitting in our checking account and a mountain of bills begging to be paid or with the gift of time on my side.

If I have a fully funded emergency fund, I know that when something tragic happens, I will have time. I will have time to grieve and to help my children process and grieve. I will have time to find the right job in my new reality. I won't have to rush out and take the first job I find.

I know this all sounds horribly morbid, but the truth is that in life, anything can happen. We all know that now. I don't have a crystal ball and I'm not God, but I do know that life moves incredibly fast, and if you aren't prudent in your planning, you will get caught up in a tidal wave. And your emergency fund may just be what keeps you and your family from getting swept away.

Let's Make Some Money Moves

1. Determine your six-month emergency fund number by adding up all your essential expenses for one month and then multiplying it by six.

2. After calculating your six-month emergency fund number, determine what your starter emergency fund goal should be. You should be able to save this amount in about three months with serious determination and focus. If you're struggling to come up with a number for yourself, $3,000 is a good starting point. Remember to discuss this goal with your spouse and agree on working toward it together.

3. Make a plan and execute it. Plan that any and all additional money you earn or receive will immediately go into your starter emergency fund. Track your savings progress to keep you motivated to achieve your goal.

Eight

The "Secret" of Becoming Debt Free

When Pat and I started our debt-free journey, everyone thought we had completely lost our minds. They couldn't believe we were going to live on one income, pay off my student loans, and cut our spending to the bone. Then we became debt free, and friends started asking us for the "secret" of how we did it.

Since I was writing my blog and sharing on my online platforms about our family's journey toward debt freedom, I thought I had pretty much shared this so-called secret. Still, family and friends kept asking, and I realized that they thought I was holding something back. They assumed I was sharing one thing online while doing something else to make it happen. At first this confused me and even made me angry. But then

I realized where this thought process was coming from. My friends and family hoped I would tell them the easy way or the shortcut to getting out of the hot water they found themselves in financially.

The cold, hard truth is that going into debt is just like gaining weight—it is easy and mindless. However, as we all know, losing weight is incredibly hard. We love to eat whatever we want, and it takes a lot of time and effort to exercise and plan and cook healthy meals. So we end up hoping for that magical weight-loss pill that will do the hard work of shedding those dreaded pounds without ever having to lift a single dumbbell or give up a single doughnut. But oh, my friend, you and I both know the truth. You know there's no magic pill for weight loss that allows you to lounge around on your couch and eat nothing but junk food.

It's the same with debt. There's no magic pill that will make your debt go away, not even bankruptcy. For example, student loans and back-owed taxes don't go away in bankruptcy, nor is bankruptcy free. Depending on the type of bankruptcy and how much debt you're carrying, declaring bankruptcy can range anywhere from $5,000 to $15,000 or more. Bankruptcy isn't a magic fix-all pill to solve debt problems. The only way to solve that problem is to roll up your sleeves and get to work.

If you've already begun to build up a starter emergency fund, you're no stranger to hard work. Now you can use those new financial muscles to dig yourself out of the debt hole. In my opinion, it's actually easier to get out of debt than to save money. I know that sounds crazy. But something magical happens as you tackle your debt: you can't wait to see it gone and that motivates you to keep going.

Snowball versus Avalanche Methods for Debt Payment

So how should you go about paying off your debt? In general, there are two methods: the snowball method and the avalanche method. Each method has its pros and cons.

Using the *snowball method*, you list out and pay your debts in order from smallest balance to largest. In other words, you're building up a giant snowball by starting small, gaining momentum, and finally going big. Using the *avalanche method*, you list out and pay your debts in order of highest interest rate to lowest. In other words, you're avalanching down from the top interest rate to the bottom.

There's no right or wrong method for paying off debt. But I have seen many more success stories from using the snowball method than the avalanche method. The snowball method gives you quick wins that help to light a motivational fire and encourage you to keep going. With the avalanche method, you could potentially be paying off the same debt for months or even years before it's finally paid and you can move on to the next debt. So even though mathematically it does make more sense to pay the high-interest debts first, it may not make as much sense when you factor in motivation.

Math didn't make Pat and me fall into debt. Our behavior

did. We lived paycheck to paycheck, had no real idea of where our money was going, and overspent like there was no tomorrow. We knew we couldn't trust ourselves to break free from the chains of debt without changing our behavior around money. We also realized we needed to make it almost foolproof to keep the momentum going. Had we started with our highest-interest debt first, we would have started with one of my student loans, which was a beast of a loan. We would not have come even remotely close to paying it off in the five months we had before our second child was due, nor would we have been motivated to continue paying it off during the sleepless months of living with a newborn. But knocking out two credit card debts before our baby was born gave us the "win" we needed to keep going.

Now, maybe you're more comfortable with the avalanche method. That's okay. There's nothing wrong with following a different school of thought from the one Pat and I used. The key here is to make sure that no matter which debt-killing method you choose, it's the one that will keep you motivated when things get hard. Because, trust me, things will get bumpy along the debt-free journey. Just as losing weight requires sacrifice, so will getting out of debt.

The "Rule" for Becoming Debt Free

Besides choosing your method for tackling debt, you also need to commit to following one rule: stop using all forms of debt. I know following this "rule" is going to be hard for you, because it was hard for Pat and me as well. It's also going to challenge everything you've ever been told about money. But if you're truly serious about becoming and, most importantly, staying debt free, you're going to have to follow this one rule.

So stop using all forms of debt. Like right now. Yes, this means no credit cards, no new loans, no borrowing money from friends or family. I know this is hard. But it's the only way to achieve your goal of being debt free. If you have credit card debt, you need to cut up those cards. Going cold turkey is the only way to break the bad habit of relying on credit cards to pay your bills or bail you out in an emergency.

How to Kill Off Debt

No matter which debt-paying method you choose, you'll need to take specific steps to kill off your debt. By now, you should know how much debt you have accumulated. If you haven't already listed your debts, stop reading and go do that now. Total them up. Let that number sink in, because that's the mountain you're about to climb. And you're going to conquer that beast!

As stated previously, when you were building your starter emergency fund, you first determined how much money you would need to survive six months without an income. You then worked backward to determine a much easier amount to focus on. That amount became the goal for your starter emergency fund, and for the next three months or so, you focused *only* on that goal. That laser focus is what enabled you to achieve your goal.

The same principle applies here no matter which debt pay-off method you choose. You're going to focus *only* on that first debt on your list. If you choose the snowball method, you're going to start with the debt with the smallest balance. If you choose the avalanche method, you're going to start with the debt with the highest interest rate.

Step 1: Make Debt Payment a Priority in Your Budget

Look over your quick-start budget. Do you have any money you can add to your minimum payment toward that first debt on your list? If so, go ahead and pay that money. Then repeat this process every time you update your budget. If you have a regular, unchanging income, you might want to set aside a specific dollar amount each month to pay toward that debt. If you have an irregular income, use any leftover money you have each month.

Step 2: Keep Reducing Your Expenses

Remember all that cutting and reducing of expenses we did to build a starter emergency fund in chapter 7? Well, if you haven't yet worked on eliminating or reducing your expenses, today is the day to do it. The fastest way to pay off debt is to make as much room as possible in your household budget. This may require some temporary sacrifices, such as giving up subscription services or eating out, but they will be worth it in the end. (You'll hear more about sacrifice in the next chapter.) Remember why you began this journey to pay off debt and free yourself from this burden. Keeping your *why* in front of you will help motivate you when the sacrifices become hard.

STEP 3: FIND WAYS TO GENERATE ADDITIONAL INCOME

Just as we did with our starter emergency fund, again, you're going to need to find ways to generate additional cash so you can kill off that first debt on your list. This includes selling anything and everything you don't need anymore, and you may also need to think about picking up a second job, signing up for an extra shift at work, or starting your own side hustle.

Some ideas for a side hustle are teaching or tutoring online through sites such as VIPKid or Outschool. Outschool does not require a formal education in teaching. Another idea is to freelance your services. If you're an accountant by day, you can outsource your services online as a bookkeeper. If you're an administrative assistant, you can offer your services as a virtual assistant. If you're a stay-at-home mom to young children, you can offer childcare services. My best advice when figuring out a side hustle is to make a list of all the skills and talents you have and start researching how you can transfer them into services. Then find the one that works best for your skills and schedule.

STEP 4: PAY THE DEBT!

This step is obvious but all-important. You absolutely *must* pay the additional money you find, make, or earn toward your debt. Remember, you're just focusing on that first debt, but it's not going to pay off itself. You have to put action behind your goal. There isn't a book, online course, podcast, or YouTuber that's going to reach into your bank account and pay off that debt for you. You have to be the one to make it happen.

Let's Talk About Student Loans

It is estimated that nearly 45 percent of millennials have student loan debt.[2] I was once one of them, so I know firsthand how incredibly difficult killing off student loan debt can be. I could sit here and play the blame game of how my generation was essentially groomed to believe that to be successful, we *had* to go to college. As I mentioned before, I now believe a college degree is not necessary for success. But since a huge portion of my generation is suffering from this crisis, we need to talk about how to defeat those loans.

Before you can aggressively attack this debt, you must know what type of student loans you have. Are yours federal or private loans? What are the interest rates? Who owns your loans (e.g., Nelnet, Navient, Great Lakes, etc.)? Are they consolidated? The problem with federal loans is that they can sometimes look like they are consolidated when they really aren't. You make one single payment, and then that loan holder (for me, it was Nelnet) divvies up the payment according to each loan's minimum payment. A truly consolidated student loan means you have only one loan with one balance and one payment.

My student loans were just under $30,000 when we started the debt-free journey in 2013, and they were the last of our consumer debts that we killed off. I would have liked to have moved this debt to the front of the line, but the truth is, we did not have the means to pay it off quickly without first having made room in our budget by paying off the other smaller debts.

Honestly, I didn't think it was possible to pay it off early. I once made an extra payment on my loans only to find out that, since I had not specified which loan to apply the money to, they not only divvied it up among all my loans but the interest took the majority of that payment! Talk about sapping one's motivation.

If you want to make killing off those student loans a reality, you'll need to contact the loan company and find out at what time your loans accrue new interest. For me, my loans would accrue more interest at 1:00 p.m. Pacific Time. That meant I had to make my additional debt-killing payments by then to avoid having my extra payments get eaten up by more interest. You'll need to do the same if you don't want this happening to you. After finding out by what time you must make those extra payments, you'll also need to find out your specific loan holder's process for handling additional payments made.

I would log in, select the smallest student loan, and make a payment specific to that one loan as an extra payment. Over time, as each smaller student loan was paid off, I had lowered the overall minimum payment required on the loans. That meant I now had even more debt-killing power because I could pay the difference toward the next smallest loan. I continued this process until I had killed off my entire student loan debt.

Your specific situation may be different from mine since student loans vary. The point is, it's important to find out all the specifics about your loans. You will then know how best to attack them and quickly pay them off.

A Word to the Wise

No one taught Pat and me how to become debt free, and the truth is, I can't teach you either. When it comes to paying off debt, just like losing weight, I can hand you all the tools you need to do it, but it is up to you to put them into action.

If you had told me seven years ago—a terrified, pregnant mama—that we would be debt free, own our home outright, and be able to live without financial fear, I wouldn't have believed you. I was afraid, and for a while, I was paralyzed by that fear. Living free of any form of debt seemed unbelievable. At that time, I didn't know anyone who didn't have a credit card payment, car loan (or two), boat loan, or mortgage. I only knew that when it came time to buy a car, you went to the dealership, traded in your old one, and signed on the dotted line for a new one, praying you could afford the payments every month. I had no idea that a debt-free life was possible. It took moving past my paralyzing fear and taking those first steps to get across the finish line.

If you want the freedom and security of a debt-free life, my dear friend, then you, too, are going to have to quit relying on credit cards and loans to save you in times of need. You're going to have to work hard, sell off a few things, reduce your spending, and pay off debt. If you do that, you'll cross that finish line faster than you ever believed you could.

Let's Make Some Money Moves

1. Decide which debt payoff method you will use: snowball method or avalanche method.
2. List your debts in order, according to the debt payoff method you chose.
3. Review your quick-start budget to determine if there is any wiggle room. If so, pay that money toward the first debt on your list.
4. List ways you can generate additional income, such as selling off things you no longer need or want, starting a side hustle, picking up overtime, and so on.
5. Immediately apply any additional income received, such as a bonus or tax refund, toward the debt you're currently working on.
6. If you have student loans, research the terms of your loans and make payments in a way that maximizes your ability to kill off that debt.

Nine

SACRIFICE EQUALS SUCCESS

I've already told you that there's no "secret" to becoming debt free and financially stable, but that may have been a bit of a lie. It's true that there's really not a secret, per se, but there is a really big catch: you won't achieve financial success without sacrifice.

Our family's journey toward financial freedom came with its fair share of sacrifices, including, as I mentioned, picking up dog poop. But for me, this journey came with a hard-hitting sucker punch to my pride that I wasn't expecting.

I am the poster child for the American belief that "you are what you drive." It wasn't that I had to have a luxury car like a Mercedes. I just had to have a nice car. It didn't have to be brand new, but it sure needed to look like it was. In 2013, I was driving around in my dream car: a fully loaded 2008 Chevy Tahoe. I had finally made it! My dream car came complete with built-in navigation, a TV system for the kids, wood grain on the dash, and heated seats. You name it, the car had it. I loved that Tahoe—but it came with a hefty car loan. Granted, at the time we signed on the dotted line for that car loan, we were thinking only in terms of payment: "Can we afford the payment every month?" I had already run the numbers and determined, "Yes! We can."

But I had forgotten that my student loans were going to be due within a year, and we were going to have to start making the minimum payments. I also failed to realize that we would have more children. Granted, our middle child came as a surprise, and we weren't really expecting to start and end 2012 pregnant. But that's the trouble with thinking in terms of monthly payments instead of total debt. You fail to account for the variable that is life. Life will happen, and if you dig yourself too deep of a hole, it can feel nearly impossible to climb out.

Pat and I were 100 percent on board with paying off our "stupid" debts—the credit cards—before our middle child was born. But we had not yet truly planned anything beyond that. We achieved our goal of paying off those credit cards only a few days before our son was born, and we thought we would be able to breathe a little easier. But then Pat took a new job where his benefits came out of his paycheck every week. Even though he was making the same amount of money, because of his benefits, we were actually receiving less money to live on every month.

By the end of 2013, we found ourselves in the same predic-ament we'd been in at the beginning of the year. Even though we no longer had any credit card debt, we still had debts. My Tahoe payments and student loans were eating up a consider-able amount of Pat's paycheck every month. I was still walking dogs and blogging as my side hustle, but they were no longer providing enough to kill off our remaining debts as fast as we needed them to.

One day Pat suggested I get rid of my Tahoe and pay cash for another car. God bless that sweet man, because I don't believe he truly understood the crazy that he was in for when he made that simple suggestion. I couldn't believe he would suggest such a thing! Not only was the Tahoe my dream car, but it was also safe and reliable. And now he wanted to stick me in an older car? Oh no. Not happening.

Three months later, we were still struggling, and I had my "come to Jesus" moment. I had to face the truth that my pride was killing us financially. I knew in my heart something had to give. I tried with my accounting wizardry to make the numbers work, telling myself that we could find a way to pay off that Tahoe quickly. Maybe if we just hustled more, we could do it. Maybe if we refinanced for a lower interest rate, we could kill it off faster and I could still keep the car. But nothing worked. The truth was right there in my spreadsheet. I could either hold on to the Tahoe—the very thing that was dragging my family down—or I could let it go.

On my birthday in 2014, we spent the entire day driving around metro Atlanta going to various car dealerships. Even though we now had some money in savings, we didn't know if it was enough to buy a car. We were trying to find a dealer willing to take the Tahoe for what we owed on it (or close to what we owed on it), who also had a car we could afford to pay outright. We finally found this unicorn of a car dealer, and Pat picked out a 2001 Toyota Sequoia that changed colors like a mood ring. It was (and still is) purple in my opinion, but the dealer kept saying it was "thunder gray," whatever that meant. The only bells and whistles this car had were leather seats and a sunroof. No heated seats, no TVs in the back, and no built-in navigation. There wasn't even an auxiliary port to plug in my phone! I mean, how was I going to listen to my custom playlists? Oh, but it did have a cassette player, so I could theoretically play my old mixtapes from the nineties. There were rust spots and so many dings, scratches, and dents on the rear bumper I swear whoever drove the car previously didn't know how to back up and just hit everything in sight.

As we pulled away in our "new" car I bawled like a baby. I couldn't believe I had just written the check for this car. I had just given up my dream car for a car that was a far cry from dreamy. In fact, as some family members declared (to my agreement), "Jessi, that's the ugliest car you've ever owned."

But—and this is a huge but—we *owned* it. No more loan hanging over our heads. No more $441 monthly payments. To my surprise, I discovered that not having a car loan felt like getting the biggest pay raise ever!

Now, maybe you're reading this story of my temper tantrum about a car and rolling your eyes at how silly I was. But

I'm willing to bet there's something in your life that matters a lot to you, and if you were asked to give it up, you'd have a similar reaction. For some people the size of their home matters. For others it's the glamorous vacations. For still others it's their children's extracurricular activities. We all have something that would be hard to give up. For me, it was my car. I didn't realize until the moment I gave up the Tahoe for the Sequoia just how much of my identity I had wrapped up in the car I drove. I'm pretty certain no one else cared, but for me, letting go of that status symbol was difficult.

No Pain, No Gain

If you follow #thedebtfreecommunity on social media, you're bound to find posts about giving up stuff. You'll see everything from giving up that morning coffee at Starbucks to giving up a house and moving the family of ten into an RV. That's because, in order to gain financial freedom, you're going to have to decide what is worth giving up and what is worth keeping.

I don't share the Tahoe story or other stories to make you feel like you have to dump your car or move out of your 2,500-square-foot home and into a 300-square-foot RV. I share it because you, too, may run into a big stumbling block on your financial journey. And that stumbling block just may be of your own creation, and it could be the very thing keeping you from achieving your ultimate goal.

Chances are you already know that such a stumbling block

exists. You may know that your Amazon habit is completely wrecking your household budget. You may know that your fountain Diet Coke obsession is draining away your excess cash. Or maybe your stumbling block is something bigger—like a car, a rental property, a boat, or even a primary residence. The truth is, we're human and we have wants. In and of themselves, our wants aren't bad things. They only become "bad" when we allow them to rule over us.

Here's what I mean. My car saga is real. I still go through phases when that Sequoia isn't "good enough" anymore, and I start eyeing Suburbans that are a decade newer. Granted, we now have the cash to pay outright for a newer (albeit not fancy) Suburban. I'm not wrong for wanting a newer car; after all, soon my car will turn twenty years old. But I need to put that want in perspective compared to my other goals and dreams. Yes, we may have the cash, but taking that much out of our savings would leave us with a much smaller safety net. The question becomes: Do I really want to trade the security of money in the bank for the status symbol of a newer car? Nope. I love my security more than I desire a new car.

Of course, at some point the Sequoia will cost more to repair than it is worth, and it will be wiser financially to take that money from our savings to buy a newer car. But that time is not now. Right now, a newer car is a want, not a need. Putting my wants into perspective by focusing on my goals helps me to make the right choices for my family. That is the point of sacrifice on the debt-free journey. You need to determine for you and for your family what is worth giving up. You decide what you truly need versus what you only want. And when you focus on your needs first, you will make headway. I promise.

Picking Your "Hard"

It can be hard to see past the present, and the very thought of having to give up something can be difficult, especially when everything feels hard right now. I know that feeling well. I also know that we each have to pick our "hard."

It's hard to stick to a budget, but it's also hard living paycheck to paycheck. It's hard to save money, but it's also hard when your car needs a major repair and you don't have the cash to pay for it. It's hard paying off debt, but it's also hard not having any money left over from your paycheck after paying the bills. It's hard saving for retirement and not touching it for decades, but it's also hard when your body can no longer physically work long hours while you've got bills to pay and no retirement saved up. The truth is, you'll have to pick your hard. I'm not here to shame you. Your version of hard will be very different from mine, but that doesn't make it any less or more hard. It's *all* hard.

If you've made any of the money moves recommended in this book, you've already done a whole lot of hard work, so go ahead and give yourself a pat on the back. Most people would have quit by now—but not you.

Whenever I face a challenge, I inspire myself with quotes from those who have achieved greatness. One of my favorite quotes is from basketball player Kobe Bryant, who said, "Great things come from hard work and perseverance. No excuses."[3] This quote is on a sticky note on my laptop because writing this book is hard. When the words are hard to write or I need to scrap whole chapters and start over because they don't serve you well, I look at this quote and I'm reminded that no one is going to show up to do this for me. If I fail, it's on me, not you or anyone else. I can't give up. I have to persevere and do the hard work of writing. No excuses. And even if I don't write a bestseller, when this book is finished and published, I will have succeeded.

In the same way, on your journey to being debt free, you only fail when you give up. Sure, you may not hit all your goals in the time frame you want, but that's okay. We didn't meet our deadlines either. It took us two months longer than we had planned to pay off all our consumer debt. It took us a year longer than we had anticipated to pay off our house. It took us four months longer than we had hoped to save up a six-month emergency fund. If we had stopped just because we didn't hit our deadline, we would not be in the position we are in today. You only fail when you give up. Period.

So when you're faced with hard choices on this journey, remind yourself of the hard things you've already done. In fact, if you need to, write them down. If you don't think you've done something hard, let me ask you, do you have a driver's license? If so, you've done something incredibly hard. You learned how to drive a machine that is bigger and heavier than you and that could quite possibly harm you or someone else. Yet now, when you get in the car, without thinking about it, you can put the car in reverse and back up without checking what position your mirrors are in or making sure your hands are on ten and two. You've already done something hard; you learned how to drive. And I know that's not the only hard thing you've ever done or learned how to do. Give yourself some credit.

Redefine Comfort

Now I'm going to switch gears and come out and say something that's probably going to sting. As Americans we're used to comfort and comfortable living. I know you have probably experienced discomfort and maybe even found yourself on more than one occasion, like I have, with a declined credit card at the grocery store. But I still stand pretty firm in my belief that most of us are living in comfort.

Hear me out. Not only are we more materially blessed than most of the entire world's population—we can turn a knob and have safe water to drink—we also have incredible opportunities that for centuries have encouraged immigrants, like my great-grandparents, to move here to seek a better life for their families.

In the United States, our perception of comfort is a little distorted. Long before we were even thinking of becoming debt free, Pat and I went on vacation to St. Lucia and stayed at a gorgeous five-star resort. One day we went on an excursion that involved a two-hour drive. At one point we stopped to get gas and use the restroom, and we found ourselves with a twenty-minute break in the heart of a slum. I had seen slums and dire poverty on TV before, but nothing could have prepared me for what it's like to be standing in the midst of one.

I watched children playing in the sewer gutter with no clothes on and mothers trying to wash laundry in the same sewer water. In an attempt to make myself feel better, I convinced Pat to walk with me to what appeared to be an abandoned graveyard and Catholic church. I will never forget the moment I pushed open the doors of that old church. I immediately noticed a huge hole in the roof where I could see the sky. Inside, Mass was going on and the church was packed.

I broke down and cried. How could these people—living in conditions worse than that of the homeless men and women at the shelter where I had volunteered a year earlier—have faith this strong? Here they were, giving thanks to God for what little they had, when I, a woman barely making $20,000 a year, had so much more than they did. At that moment I came face-to-face with the reality of how comfortable my life really was. I had a washing machine that washed my clothes in clean water—clean enough that I could actually drink it if I needed to.

Now, I'm not sharing this story with you to make you feel bad about the fact that, here in the United States, we are incredibly blessed with the comforts we enjoy. I'm sharing this with you because we must redefine what our culture has sold us as what we're supposed to have. What you may feel is a sacrifice may not be that much of a sacrifice at all.

Finding Things for Cheap or Free

As you build up your ability to do hard things, one of the things you'll need to learn is to give up instant gratification. We are so used to having our needs and desires fulfilled with the click of a mouse that waiting any longer than two "Amazon Prime shipping" days can seem like an eternity. But if you learn to wait and employ some creativity, effort, and prayer, you may be able to find what you need for cheap or even free!

For instance, let's say that you really need a new dresser for one of your children. You can head online or to your local furniture store and pay upwards of $300 or more for a brand-new dresser. However, if your children are anything like mine, that dresser won't look so new by the end of the year. Instead, you can sacrifice a little and do your best to be patient. Ask around—neighbors, friends, family, online—for anyone looking to get rid of a dresser. You may have to wait longer, but I promise, you'll find someone willing to let go of a dresser for cheap or even for free.

When we started homeschooling during the pandemic, I needed something to store all our supplies. They were literally piled in a corner on the floor in my dining room, and it was driving me crazy. I was beyond tempted to buy one of those really cute cubbies all the cool Pinterest moms had in their fancy homeschool rooms, which costs around $500. But to do that I would have had to give up our goal of maxing out our Roth IRA contributions. So, instead, I asked around. Wouldn't you know it? A woman from our church had an older cubby that was still in mint condition, even though she had used it for ten years homeschooling her children. She sold it to me for twenty-five dollars! Yes, for weeks I lived with a messy, disorganized dining room that drove me nuts. But the waiting was worth it. I now have an organized space that didn't cost us our retirement goals.

Using No-Spend Months

I'll be honest, it's no fun not spending money. Yes, I'm a saver and I love big bank accounts, but I'm also human. I was brought up in consumer culture, so I have wants and an Amazon wish list a mile long. But if you want to really put some pep in your step and make progress with your money goals, few things will get you there faster than a no-spend month.

The idea behind a no-spend month is to raise your money awareness by severely restricting your spending. A no-spend month is both easier and harder than it seems. The ground rules are:

1. No spending on anything that isn't a bill or groceries. (Eating out doesn't count as groceries.)
2. Don't fret over how much you are or are not saving. The point isn't to save money but to change your spending habits.

That's it. You still put gas in your car so you can go to work, but instead of stopping at the local drive-through for a coffee and biscuit, you drive straight to work. The purpose is to help you understand where you spend your money. It will also help you develop the habit of being aware of your spending. Trust me, nothing makes you more hyperaware of your spending than telling yourself you can't spend any money.

If you have an overflowing pantry and freezer, or if you find that you are "cheating" by spending more than you should at the grocery store, you can eliminate all or most of your grocery shopping during your no-spend month. As many of us found out during the pandemic shutdown, scarcity can inspire creativity in the kitchen! Challenge yourself to go a week without going to the grocery store and start using up the excess you have!

Speaking of the pandemic, I'd bet the shutdowns already showed you that you can drastically cut your spending. Many of us were forced to give up a lot of the things we enjoy, such as eating out, travel, movies, concerts, plays, gym workouts, manicures, and even haircuts. Think back on those months. If you made it through that, you can certainly make it through one month of no spending!

The point of a no-spend month is not to make you miserable. The point is simply to make you aware of your spending habits so you can make positive changes. Of course, a no-spend month will help you get even closer to achieving your financial goals, because you can throw all the money you're not spending toward it. This will ignite the motivational fire that will bring you closer to what you want to achieve.

Practical Sacrifices

Maybe you're like me and need someone to kindly suggest, as Pat did with the Tahoe, a sacrifice that may be in your best interest. Now, hear me loud and clear: you and your family need to decide for yourselves what to sacrifice. But I'm listing some suggestions here for your convenience. A few of these suggestions may make sense to you and others may not. You decide.

- Cancel TV cable/satellite subscription or streaming services.
- Scale back vacations or halt them altogether.
- Give up the fancy phone for a less desirable model and a cheaper plan.
- Trade in the car with a loan for an older one you can pay cash for.
- Sell your home and either rent a place (for less than the mortgage you were paying) or buy a cheaper home.
- Move somewhere with a lower cost of living.
- Take a second job or find a side hustle.
- Give up restaurant visits or takeout and cook at home.
- Live off a smaller portion of your income or switch from living off two incomes to one.
- Delay purchases until you have cash to pay for them.

- Shop at secondhand stores for clothes and household items or ask around to see if you can get something cheaper or for free.
- Limit your children's extracurricular activities.
- Embark on a no-spend month.

I encourage you to make your own list of potential sacrifices that may serve your family. If you're married, talk with your spouse about it. Your spouse more than likely will have their own opinions on what sacrifices are worth it and what are not. Work together to come up with a plan and execute it together.

A quick word about the sacrifice of working a job you don't love. I'm certainly not suggesting you continue working at a job where you are unsafe. But both Pat and I have had to work jobs we didn't love in order to achieve our goal. Use the dissatisfaction you feel for the job as motivation. We both discovered that the job not only became more tolerable when we had an end in sight, but it actually became more enjoyable, like a secret game. If you're working at a job you don't love, but it pays the bills and can help you achieve your goal, keep going. Set a goal and put a smile on your face, because you're on a mission.

Truth be told, all goals require sacrifices. It doesn't matter if it's a money goal, a workout goal, or a business goal. The point of the sacrifice is not pain but knowing what you really want and what you're willing to let go of to achieve that goal. You get to decide what is and what is not important. Great things are ahead. No more excuses.

Let's Make Some Money Moves

1. Name your stumbling block, then have your spouse name theirs. How will you address these roadblocks to your financial goals?

2. List all the hard things you've already accomplished in your life. Post this list where you can see it when you find yourself in need of a little motivation.

3. What mindset do you need to change to make progress on your financial journey? Do you need to redefine what is "hard" or rethink what "comfort" means?

4. List some sacrifices—temporary or permanent—you can make to achieve your financial goals. If you're married, be sure to discuss this topic with your spouse and get their input and buy-in.

Ten

GETTING AND STAYING
OUT OF DEBT

It was 2013, and we had just saved $3,000 in our starter emergency fund. Determined to become debt free before the birth of our second child, we decided our next step was to pay off our credit card debt of $4,000. We knew we would never get out of credit card debt if we kept using our credit cards. So we made the dramatic decision to cut up our credit cards, vowing never to rely on credit again. When others found out what we did, they responded with thoughts that echoed their own limiting beliefs about money: "You need a credit card for emergencies. Don't be fools. You're parents."

I won't tell you who said these unwise words to Pat and me, but I will give them grace because I know they were just sharing a very common sentiment in the world of personal finance. Credit cards seem like a necessity, especially if you have children. As parents, Pat and I try very hard to care for our children and to provide for them well. But I hardly think that having a credit card makes you a good parent. In fact, I believe the best thing we ever did for our children was to take that very scary step of cutting up our credit cards.

A mere five months later, our family tree changed. Not only did we have another son, but we were also learning to live without credit cards. We went from hardly ever discussing money to daily having fruitful conversations on how we were doing financially. We went from never knowing where our money went to having a plan for every dollar. We went from swiping our credit cards to save us, to having liquid cash on hand as our safety net.

Granted, all this didn't happen overnight. But by taking that drastic step of cutting up our credit cards, we not only got out of debt but *stayed* out of debt.

The Danger of Debt

Debt eats your income. Read that again. *Debt eats your income.* It doesn't matter if your paycheck is $500 a week or $5,000 a week. If you have debt, it will eat the money you just went to work all week to earn. Don't believe me? Stop right now and go tally up exactly how much you pay every month in the form of minimum payments. Don't even include your mortgage if you have one; just tally up the minimum payments on your credit cards, personal loans, car loans, student loans, and any money you owe family or friends.

For Pat and me, at one point our minimum debt payment total was nearly $900 a month, not including the mortgage payment. You know what that meant? After making those minimum payments, we had a little more than $2,000 a month to live on. And oh, we still had to pay the mortgage payment of $709. That means we had less than $1,500 to buy groceries, pay utilities, and live life.

Tallying up how much we were paying every month in minimum payments provided the catapult that launched us on the debt-free journey. Granted, when we started, our main focus was on the credit cards, because they were the lowest-balance debts we had. Once we paid those off, we gained momentum, which helped us to keep going until we finally crossed the finish line.

Back in the Hole

When Pat and I got married in 2009, we both brought debt into our marriage. To get rid of that debt, we thought it would be a fantastic idea to take on a debt-consolidation loan.

This was long before we ever dreamed of being debt free. In fact, the phrase "debt free" didn't even exist in our minds. We didn't even know it was something you could achieve. We were simply trying to get rid of Pat's truck loan and credit card bills and my many overused credit cards from my single years. At the time, we each decided to keep one credit card open, one in Pat's name and one in mine. The whole scenario played out well on paper. We were consolidating roughly $15,000 of total debt with only one interest rate to contend with! And better yet, we could have it paid off in three years.

Thankfully, Pat and I did pay it off in three years, but here's where we ran into trouble: In those three years, we had not yet developed the habits needed to manage money together. We had not yet learned how to live off our paychecks. We were still living life as if we had all the money in the world. So very quickly we found ourselves back in the hole, owing money on those two still-open credit cards. Because we had not yet developed the habits and disciplines necessary for controlling our money, our overspending and mindlessness took over once more. We tried to find the fastest route possible to free ourselves from the bind we put ourselves in yet again, but we ended up creating a whole new one.

The difference between 2009 Pat and Jessi and 2013 Pat and Jessi is that, in 2013, we committed ourselves to learning, trying, and maybe even failing to figure out how to manage money. We stopped looking for the quick fixes to our problems and instead spent many days in the trenches working together to climb our way out. We worked hard to develop the habits and disciplines needed to not just get out of debt but also *stay* out of debt.

The 2009 Pat and Jessi thought they had made the best move by consolidating their debts—and in some ways they had—but the reality was, because they lacked the skill sets to stay in a better position, they fell backward. That's what happens when we try to run before we can walk or try to walk before we learn to crawl. We have to be willing to make the small changes that lead to the big changes that lead to the life-long changes. And one of those small changes was to cut up those credit cards.

Still Swiping? Cut It Out!

We've already discussed the two methods for paying off debt: the snowball method and the avalanche method. And you may have already jumped right into paying off your debts from smallest to largest, as we advised. Hurray! But have you cut up your credit cards? The truth is, you're never going to be debt free if you're still relying on debt. If you're still swiping the other credit cards while you're trying to pay off the one with the smallest balance, you're digging yourself into a bigger hole. To avoid sinking further into debt and further away from the freedom of living without the burden of debt, you're going to have to stop using those credit cards.

Perhaps you have played the shell game of moving one credit card balance to another credit card to get a lower introductory rate. But this, as with our debt-consolidation loan, only tricks you into believing that things will improve. At the end of the day, if you don't cut up the other cards or keep yourself from swiping the new card, you really haven't helped yourself much at all. It's not the interest rate that's killing you. It's your behavior. You'll never get rid of consumer debt if you don't look in the mirror at the consumer who is causing it!

What exactly is consumer debt? Consumer debt is any and all debts you have other than your mortgage. This includes your car loan, credit card debt, personal loans, wedding loans, student loans, the money you owe your mama, and so on.

Why is paying off consumer debt so important? Because it's eating away at your wealth-building potential. The majority of your paycheck is going right back out the door to all your minimum payments. In other words, your debt is a liability, a ball and chain dragging around your ankles and slowing your momentum.

You have probably heard the terms *assets* and *liabilities*. The assets are the things that represent money—home, car, checking and savings accounts, and retirement accounts— and the liabilities are the debts you have attached to those assets. The goal is to always have greater assets than liabilities. Unfortunately, most people end up with the reverse; more liabilities, or debt, than they do assets. Paying off your consumer debt not only helps you keep more of your money every paycheck but also makes sure that your assets are worth more than the debts attached to them.

Here are a few more debt terms that are important to know. A *secured loan* is a debt that has something physical behind it that can be repossessed if you are unable to pay the loan, such as mortgages and car loans. An *unsecured loan* has no collateral behind it, such as credit card loans, personal loans, and student loans. Typically, unsecured loans charge higher interest and are only given to those who have decent credit scores.

Now, here's where things get interesting. We have been taught to get a credit card in order to build our credit score, and then guard our credit score with our very life. So when I tell people they should cut up their credit cards to get out of debt and *stay* out of debt, they protest: "But what about my credit score?" So let's take a look at that.

Why Do I Have to Cut Up My Credit Cards?

A credit score is a measure of how well you pay off debt. As personal finance expert Dave Ramsey says, credit scores are "I love debt" scores.[4] Credit scores go up when you use credit and then pay off your bills each month, and they go down if you don't pay your credit card bills. The problem is, they also go down if you don't use credit cards at all.

Shortly after we paid off our home in 2019, our credit scores fell. Personally, my credit score fell to the lowest it has ever been in my life. And even though I wanted to put on a bold face and say it was no big thing because we were debt free and didn't plan on borrowing money anytime soon, it was really hard to see that number fall. At that point, I had been living without a single credit card for more than six years. Not only was I not using credit cards, but I didn't even have one to use if I wanted to! This all contributed to my credit score falling, because I now had zero debts and no open lines of credit. So I decided to do a little experiment. I wanted to see how fast I could improve my now sad credit score and if I could use credit cards again without falling back into temptation to overspend.

For this experiment, I had to open a line of credit. I chose an Amazon Prime credit card and put thirty dollars on the card. Almost instantaneously my credit score went up. If that doesn't confirm the whole "I love debt score" thing, I don't know what does. But here's what I realized after not having a credit card for six years and then opening one: it's way too easy to mindlessly swipe a credit card and fall back into old habits. In two months' time, I found myself buying things from Amazon that I didn't need (I only thought I did). It was clear to me that my temptation to overspend was far too great with a credit card versus a debit card. As soon as my experiment was over and I shared my results on YouTube, I cut up that card and closed the account.

While I can't tell you the best way to improve your credit score, what I can tell you is that you need to be hyperaware of the temptation to spend more than necessary. Old habits die hard. This is why I believe you can't have your cake and eat it too. You can't keep your credit cards in your wallet thinking you'll be stronger than the temptation to use them. If you want to rid yourself of debt once and for all, you'll need to cut the temptation out of your life.

How We Did It

While it's true that there is no secret to becoming debt free, I also know that it can sometimes feel impossible to live without debt. So just how did our little family of five, in the metro Atlanta area, live on a salary of $47,000 a year?

It took us two years to achieve the feat of becoming consumer-debt free, to dig ourselves out of the burden of $55,000 of consumer debt. In that time, Pat and I both worked numerous side hustles, threw every extra check (rebate, bonus, or tax refund) toward our debt snowball, and gave up my fully loaded Tahoe. We hit many snags along the way and even had to push back our debt-free date. But we kept going, even when it was hard.

Let's take a minute here to look at our numbers. When we started our journey toward financial freedom, we had over $55,000 of consumer debt that included our credit cards, the Tahoe loan, and my student loans; had nothing in savings; and carried an $89,000 mortgage. You may look at our mortgage number and say, "Wow, that's so low. No wonder you were able to pay it off." But let me stop this train of thought and pour some perspective into your glass.

When we bought our house, it required a lot of renovation before we could move in. Rats had taken over the home, the drawers were completely missing from the kitchen, and both toilets were literally in pieces as if some teenager had thrown cherry bombs in them. Animal waste from the previous owners' cats and dogs had completely damaged the flooring and subfloors. Just making the home livable cost us $30,000—some of which we paid in cash and some we paid with debt. It required Pat and his best friend to sleep in our boat in the garage while they completed the renovations; I was pregnant with our first child, and Pat didn't want me in the home with the rats and animal waste and construction debris.

To add more perspective, Pat was barely making $47,000 a year while supporting three and a half people, carrying an $89,000 mortgage, and dealing with $55,000 of consumer debt. To put it another way, our debt was more than three times my husband's annual salary!

If you're still not convinced that our debt-free journey took tremendous effort, our $89,000 mortgage and $55,000 consumer debt would be equivalent to someone making $160,000 having to pay off a $400,000 mortgage and more than $100,000 of consumer debt. I share this perspective so you won't get lost in our numbers and dismiss our accomplishment.

The truth is, we could have stopped at any point. We could have decided that living debt free wasn't worth the effort and allowed ourselves to fall back into debt. But we didn't. And it paid off in the end. If you're truly committed to attaining financial freedom, I have no doubt you'll achieve it. I know this because we achieved it. Your numbers could be, and more than likely are, completely different from ours. And that's okay. Don't get caught up in the comparison trap. Just get out of debt—and stay out!

Let's Make Some Money Moves

1. Are you willing to cut up your credit cards (even if it's only temporarily)? Why or why not?

2. Add up all your assets: the current value of your home (from Zillow or other websites) and cars (check Kelley Blue Book), and the money in your checking, savings, and investment accounts. Add up all your debts: mortgage and the car, student, and credit card loans. Now subtract your debts from your assets. What is your net worth?

3. What is your plan for getting out of debt or keeping yourself and your family from falling back into debt?

Eleven

REPLACING MONEY LIES
WITH MONEY TRUTHS

All my troubles would be over if I could just win the lottery.

Have you ever told yourself a money lie? I bet you have. And maybe you even believe that money lie about the lottery—that just winning the lottery would solve all your troubles. After all, the lottery wouldn't exist if people didn't believe in it!

But if you've lived a little (or read *People* magazine), you've probably heard a story of a Mega Millions lottery winner who lost it all—spending it foolishly, giving it away to family and friends, living it up. Sadly, some lottery winners are completely unprepared for their winnings. Trust me, friend: if you can't hang on to $10 when you're broke making $30,000 a year, you won't be able to hold on to $10,000 making $300,000 a year, and you may even have trouble hanging on to millions of dollars you won in the lottery! That's because without proper disciplines, habits, and mindsets in place, it will be hard to achieve the goals and dreams you're working toward, no matter how much money you make (or win). Thinking that winning the lottery will save you is one money lie we tell ourselves.

Another common money lie is: *I can't budget.* Have you ever made a budget and then promptly forgotten about it or messed it up in some way? You can bet I have made that mistake more than once, and guess what? I still make mistakes budgeting. You want to know why I still make mistakes even though I've been living a real life on a budget for nearly a decade with the discipline of a hopeful saint? Because I'm human. Because my husband is human. Because we're not perfect. Because we're not robots. But making mistakes is no reason to lie and tell ourselves that we can't budget. No one—and I mean absolutely no one—is born knowing how to budget. Sure, some folks are born into wealthy families, but that doesn't mean they know how to properly manage money.

At some point in your financial journey you're going to hit a major internal roadblock, a mindset that will derail you if you're not careful. Just like the Devil likes to lie to us and tell us all sorts of things that aren't true, we like to lie to ourselves too. We can be our own greatest enemy on our path to debt-free success. You may be telling yourself, *I can't pay off debt, I only make $30,000 a year!* But I would challenge you to change your way of thinking. When you think you can't do something, you're giving yourself an excuse—an escape route—from doing the hard work required to make the changes you want to see in your life. And since this feeling of "can't" and other lies will at some point creep up on you while you try to make the most out of your finances, I want to help you identify and reject some of those lies now, so you can replace them with money truths when they come up.

The Money Lies We Tell Ourselves

Money Lie 1: It's not enough.
Money Truth 1: Starting small is better than not
    starting at all.

If you believe the money you have is not enough to help you achieve your goal, you are killing your progress even before you start. If you want to retire one day, save for your emergency fund, or pay off the six figures of debt you've accumulated, you are going to have to start somewhere. And starting small is better than not starting at all.

For example, Pat and I chipped away at our debt five dollars at a time. Anytime we had an extra five dollars in the budget, we immediately applied it toward the current debt we were working on. Of course, five dollars at a time wasn't the only amount we paid toward our debt. The point is, we started building a habit of putting money straight toward our debt anytime there was anything left over in the budget, even if it was only five dollars. Once we were debt free, the extra money went to savings, and then eventually to paying off the mortgage. Now that money goes to our retirement.

Many people balk at the idea of five-dollar payments because to them that's nothing. They think, *Sure, it may buy me a Red Bull or a venti latte at Starbucks, but what is five bucks going to do for my financial future?* It can do a lot. In fact, in some ways, it can do more for your financial future than thousands of dollars. The habit of putting five dollars toward your debt instead of buying snacks at the convenience store can take you from financially falling behind to financially succeeding.

It's easy to get overwhelmed looking at the huge mountain of debt in front of you, but you'll never climb that mountain if you don't take the first step. Martin Luther King Jr. is often quoted as having said, "You don't have to see the whole staircase to take the first step." He's right. You don't have to see the full path in front of you to begin the journey; you simply must be willing to take the steps necessary to get you to your goal. If all you have extra this week from your budget after payday is five dollars, then put that to work for your future self and put a smile on your face, because you just did more with five dollars than most people do with fifty.

Money Lie 2: Budgets are for broke people.
Money Truth 2: Everyone needs to watch over
   their money.

Many people believe the lie that budgets are for broke people because people with money aren't counting pennies. Now granted, I'm sure to a degree that's true. People with millions in the bank likely aren't counting their pennies. But I promise you, the smart ones still know every dollar that comes in and out of their accounts and the purpose for each dollar. The truth is, you need to have your eyes on your money. You need to be aware of what your money is doing.

Someone I know didn't realize that a family member was siphoning money from them almost every day. You want to know why they didn't notice? Because they weren't paying attention to their money. This family member wasn't taking hundreds of dollars a day—they were only taking a few dollars here or there—but the amounts added up. In the end, it added up to over $3,000 before my friend caught on! Remember that whole mentality of thinking that small amounts don't add up? Well, here is a real-life example where they do. When you aren't actively watching over your money, those small amounts will find a way to disappear.

If you don't want to be broke, make your quick-start budget and stick to it. Make a regular habit of checking on your bank accounts. And for the love of everything holy, don't give people who aren't your spouse access to your money.

Money Lie 3: I made a mistake and that proves I just
    can't get it right.

Money Truth 3: The only true mistake is to quit trying.

This one is for all my beautiful fellow perfectionists out there. I can't tell you how many times I redid a budget because I didn't have it perfectly categorized. I'd get so upset when the budget didn't work out as I had planned, because I just couldn't understand how this beautiful, color-coded spreadsheet could fail me. It felt like utter betrayal.

This cycle of feeling like I could never get the budget right caused me to quit over and over again. I mean, no one likes to fail, but it's even worse when it seems as if every time you try, you fail. So I would just give up. Maybe you've done that. Maybe your budget is not working in the perfectly manicured way you planned. Maybe you haven't hit that savings goal milestone yet. Maybe you still can't decide on the "perfect" emergency fund number. No matter what it is, I promise you, there's no such thing as perfect anything when it comes to money.

To give you another example, Pat and I committed the cardinal sin in the world of personal finance. Several years ago, we cashed out my 401(k). In doing so, we not only forfeited the money itself and its future growth, but we also had to pay taxes on that money and fork over an additional 10 percent penalty for early withdrawal.

Now, every part of me doesn't want to divulge this sin. I would rather tell you that I'm perfect with money and have had only a few bumps in the road. I would love to tell you that I would never go against what my finance professors taught me or what all the financial gurus who are smarter than me preach. But I can't tell you our story without including this black mark on our financial record. Why? Because more than likely you may have done this very thing, or perhaps something even worse with your money, such as refinancing your home several times and treating your home equity more like a piggy bank instead of a wealth-building tool. But please know that the mistakes you've made don't define you. No matter what.

Mistakes, in fact, are opportunities to learn and grow. When you begin to work on your finances, you are not going to be perfect at every aspect of it, and that is 100 percent okay. You're going to have budgets that don't work. You're going to make an unbelievably stupid purchase. You're going to invest in something that loses money. When those mistakes happen, give yourself the grace you need. You are not perfect, and that is so perfectly beautiful.

When I get caught up in a vicious perfectionism cycle, I give myself permission to fail. I literally write down: "Jessi, you have permission to fail at learning how to save for retirement." And you know what? When I remember that, the pressure to be perfect rolls off and I can get back to work. The only thing I do not give myself permission to do is give up. No matter how many times I fail, I get back up and try again. No one else is going to do this hard work for me. So even though I fail, I must keep trying, otherwise it won't get done. You fail only if you stop trying or refuse to learn from mistakes.

You can even use what you've learned from your mistakes to help other people—and maybe even your own children—avoid those same mistakes. You also don't need to make mistakes yourself to learn from other people's mistakes. After all, isn't that one of the reasons you are reading this book? To get better at managing your money and avoid financial mistakes? If you spot money mistakes other people around you are making, don't disparage them or judge them, but do take note and learn. You might just save yourself a lot of money and a lot of grief.

Money Lie 4: I don't know how to do that.
Money Truth 4: With time and effort, I can learn
    how to do that.

Let me admit something. Not that long ago, I was terrified of investing. In fact, I knew very little about investing, except that I was supposed to do it. For months, I told myself I didn't know how to invest and that it was too overwhelming to learn how. So you know how much progress I made toward saving for retirement in those months? Absolutely none.

Here's the ironic part: I feared investing even though at that point in our financial journey, we were consumer-debt free and had a six-month emergency fund. I had already done some really big, scary stuff in the world of personal finance. So why was I allowing the voices in my head to tell me I couldn't figure out how to do this new, scary thing? Because fear is incredibly powerful. Fear of the unknown will always hold us back. It will convince us that we could never do that big, scary thing we know nothing about.

But you know what, friend? You're already doing something most folks would never dare dream of: you're taking control of your financial future. And even though that's scary, you're doing it. You're making money moves that are incredibly difficult. You're learning. You're tweaking. You're taking the necessary risks. Don't allow anyone—including yourself—to tell you what you can and can't do. You're smart, and with some time and effort, you can learn how to handle money. Trust that.

Money Lie 5: I don't deserve to have money.
Money Truth 5: God gives us everything we own
    and expects us to steward it wisely.

Maybe you've never suffered from the paralyzing fear of failing with something great you've been given, but I have. With great blessing comes great responsibility, and that responsibility (or the fear of it) can cause us to avoid taking action. Telling ourselves that we don't deserve it lets us feel as if we no longer have the responsibility of caring for it. Doing so makes it easy to skirt around our responsibility, because we never claimed it.

The reality is, though, we are called to be good stewards of what we've been given. No matter how much money you earn, you've been called to manage it well. Even if you don't earn six figures, you've been given responsibility over the money you earn. You've been given the duty of saving and caring for your present needs, as well as those of your future self. Whether or not you've managed to save over a million dollars for retirement, you are still responsible for using that money wisely.

In my mind, anything and everything I have—money, cars, a house, an education, family—belongs to God. He gave those things to me, and he gets to tell me how and where to use them wisely.

Money Lie 6: Being wealthy means having lots of money.
Money Truth 6: Wealth comes in many forms, and
   we are wealthier than we realize.

Let's define what it means to be wealthy. A quick Google search tells me that being wealthy is defined as having a great deal of money, resources, or assets. Therefore, being wealthy isn't 100 percent about money.

Think about it. My family not only has zero consumer debt, but we also no longer have a mortgage. We have almost a twelve-month emergency fund and max out our Roth IRA contributions every year. You might call us wealthy. However, Pat still earns just a little over $50,000 a year in income. I promise you, we don't have millions sitting in our bank account. Yet I definitely feel as if I'm wealthy because of our resources and assets. For example, I have a wealth of time. I have time with my three children. I have time with my husband. I have time to show up and help a friend in need.

Do I deserve to have this time? Yes and no. I deserve it in the sense that Pat and I worked hard to get our family to this point. So we're now reaping the fruits of that labor. But do I think that the world, the universe, the powers that be, or God himself *owes* me this wealth? No. Do I think everyone is supposed to be living this same exact life that I'm living? No. I believe everyone must define for themselves their own version of wealth.

Right now, our version is time. Our children are only in our care for a short while. Before long, they will be grown and on their own. For us, this wealth of time is more important than millions sitting in the bank. So even though we aren't millionaires, we are wealthy.

Money Lie 7: I can do it all.
Money Truth 7: Slow and steady wins the race.

If you met Pat, you'd know that the amazing man I get to call my husband is a true "I can do it all" type of guy. He works harder than anyone I've ever known and has a heart ten times the normal size. Everything he does is big. His only struggle in life is his tendency to go too hard and then burn out. Maybe you can relate to my hubby. Maybe you're just like him and you get excited about a new idea or adventure or strategy and just can't wait to do them all. So you charge out of the gate full steam ahead, only to find yourself burned out, exhausted, and maybe even having to give up halfway through because there's no gas left in the tank. This, my friend, is the other lie we tell ourselves—that we can do it all, be it all, and have it all, all the time.

If you have gone whole hog on this financial journey and are facing burnout, you may need to pump the brakes a little bit. Take a breather! If you try to do too much at once you're not going to make the kind of progress you want to achieve. Instead, give yourself some time and grace on the journey—but not too much. I know how you hardworking folks need to be pounding pavement and taking ground, so I'm not suggesting you stop completely. I'm suggesting you walk instead of run.

You see, it's tough when you are trying to build new habits and use new skill sets at the same time. You need to give yourself some room to breathe in the process. Let's say you've never been able to stick to a budget before. Your first step should be to make it your mission to stick to your quick-start budget for at least three months before moving on and adding another habit to your routine. Once you have stuck to that budget and been diligent about updating it when you stumble, you can add the next step, which is to build up your starter emergency fund. After you've achieved that goal, attack your list of debts. From there, move on to beefing up your emergency fund to six months' worth of expenses. Do it all with your normal awesome aggressiveness—just one step at a time.

The point is, Rome wasn't built in a day. You can't do it all at the same time. Be patient, work hard, and take it step by step. This is a marathon, not a sprint. Eventually, slow and steady will win the race.

Money Lie 8: I started too late.
Money Truth 8: You're right on time.

Maybe you've bought into the lie that says, *It's too late. I couldn't possibly learn how to manage money well at this age.* Or, *It's too late to start saving for retirement because I didn't start when I was in my twenties.* If you're telling yourself it's too late, I want you to pause right there. Pause and call your thought out for what it is: a limiting belief. Instead, tell yourself you are exactly where you need to be. Maybe you're not where you *want* to be, but you're where you *need* to be. You are where you are for a reason. It's not too late. No matter your age, you're right on time.

You can decide it's time for a change at any point. Don't fall into believing you can't teach old dogs new tricks, because, you know, you're not a dog. Yes, maybe it'll take you longer to save up for retirement because you started later. That's okay. Maybe it'll take more time for you to learn how to curb overspending because it's been a habit you've held on to for way too long. That's perfectly fine. It's never too late to take charge of your life and your money! When you tell yourself it's too late, you're not giving yourself grace. Tell yourself you're right on time, because, friend, you're right on time!

Money Lie 9: This is simple, so it should be easy.
Money Truth 9: This is simple, but it's not easy.

I had a friend once say to me that taking care of a newborn baby is simple. After all, if they are fed, clean, and safe, they don't ask for much else because they don't even know anything else exists! But, as we all know, caring for a newborn baby may be simple, but it is not easy.

We all know we need to break bad habits and start good ones. That's a simple truth. But the hard truth is that breaking old bad habits and establishing new good habits is not easy! Likewise, even though many aspects of personal finance are simple—such as living on less than you make—that doesn't make them easy to do.

We have a habit of confusing these two concepts and then beating ourselves up over it. If you're looking around at everyone else and wondering why you're not in XYZ place yet financially, stop. Don't look at anyone else. Instead, compare yourself only to the person you were last year. That's your competition: you. Not your neighbor or your best friend. What did you accomplish last week or last month? Was that better than the week or month before? If so, pat yourself on the back, because what you're doing may be simple, but it sure isn't easy.

Let's Make Some Money Moves

1. Take some time to listen to your own thoughts. Do you notice a mindset that may be hindering you from making the kind of progress you want? For example, are you beating yourself up over not sticking to the budget? Do you feel like you're not smart enough or self-disciplined enough to succeed? The purpose behind this exercise is to get you to identify thoughts that are hindering you or slowing you down. The only way to fix a faulty mindset is to identify it.

2. Do one thing today that you've been putting off in your finances. Do you need to transfer to savings that extra ten dollars you found when you updated the budget? Do it now.

3. What money lie mentioned in this chapter do you unconsciously believe? What truth do you need to replace it with, and how will that truth affect your attitude and behavior?

4. Take a moment and compare yourself to where you were a month or a year ago. Where have you made progress financially? Write it down and celebrate!

Twelve

FULLY FUNDED AND FREE— EVEN IN AN EMERGENCY

August 15, 2015, marked the day Pat and I achieved our goal of becoming consumer-debt free when we paid off the very last of my student loans. We also had roughly $3,000 in our starter emergency fund, and a third baby on the way. All our debts except for the house were gone, and we finally had more money coming in than going out. Life was great. Until suddenly it wasn't.

Ash Wednesday, February 10, 2016, was one of the scariest days of my entire life. Pat was working the graveyard shift out of town, and I was stuck at home due to an ice storm with a four-year-old, two-year-old, and newborn baby. I was beyond exhausted. During a feeding session with my baby, I noticed that she was irritable and the way she was breathing seemed off. My maternal alarm bell went off, signaling that I needed to get my daughter to the doctor.

By the time I walked into the doctor's office with my three children in tow, my daughter was struggling to breathe. I knew things were not good when the doctor came in, took me by the hand, and told me to leave my two older children at his office and take my daughter next door to the emergency room. Watching my newborn have her arms splinted and taped so she couldn't pull out the IVs was heartrending. Even worse was having to walk out the hospital doors without her several hours later.

My mom had picked up the boys from the doctor's office and was going to look after them overnight. My house was almost an hour away from the hospital and my mom's house was twenty minutes from the hospital in the opposite direction, but my boys had no change of clothes or special lovies with them to make spending the night with Grammy easier. So I had to drive home, pack bags for my boys and myself, drive to my mom's to drop them off, and then go back to the hospital. All the while, Pat was four and a half hours away in South Carolina. By the time I walked out the hospital doors at eleven o'clock that night, I was spent.

Have you ever been soul tired? Like your actual soul has taken a beating? That was me walking out of the hospital, leaving my baby girl behind so I could care for my other two children. What's that saying? A mother's work is never done?

No, it is not. But, by the grace of God, Pat called me as I was headed to my mom's house to say he was on his way to the hospital to stay with our daughter. Pat had been working the graveyard shift for months, so staying up all night didn't faze him. It was a blessed relief to no longer be carrying this burden alone. Thankfully, our daughter recovered quickly and was able to come home the next afternoon. Apparently, all she needed was Daddy because her breathing got better soon after he arrived.

Later I found out that Pat's boss originally wasn't going to let him leave even though we were facing a family medical emergency. But Pat stood his ground and risked being fired, and his boss finally let him leave.

This moment was our turning point. It was clear that Pat's job had to change. But he didn't want to just leave one corporate job for another. When we were first married, Pat was a small business owner for about a year, and he had a dream of doing it again. However, there was just one issue: we were still a one-income family, and even though my blog had finally started making money, we needed more security before Pat could take a leap of faith and quit his job. It was finally time for us to get serious and build up our six-month emergency fund.

It's Time to Get Serious

Chances are, if you asked someone who has become consumer-debt free and also has a fully funded emergency fund which one was harder to achieve, they would answer that saving money was harder than paying off debt. I know for us this is true. Saving money was incredibly hard, which is why we stalled for so long before we took action.

Even though paying off debt was also hard, saving money is a different kind of hard—even for savers. I believe it's because there's no real threat involved. I mean, think about it. If you don't pay your water bill, eventually the water will get turned off. If you don't pay your car loan, eventually the car will get repossessed. There's a real threat involved when you don't pay someone the money you owe them. But not paying money to yourself? There's no looming threat to that. It takes an incredible amount of discipline to keep yourself motivated and achieve your goal.

So how do you get serious about saving when the burden of debt is gone and you're finally able to breathe again? How do you force yourself to save money and keep going when all you want to do is sit and rest? The secret is this: find something worth saving for. You have to find the *why*.

We needed a fully funded emergency fund so Pat could leave his job and start his own business. Your *why* may be different. Maybe you and your spouse just found out that you're expecting your first child and desire for one of you to stay home while your children are young. Maybe you're self-employed and know you need an extra cushion for the down times. Maybe you live far away from your aging parents and want to have enough money to take time off from work to care for them in a crisis. Maybe you simply want to reduce the anxiety and tension in your home. Trust me, nothing eases financial tension like having the security of thousands of dollars in the bank.

Stop right here and identify why having a fully funded, six-month emergency fund would benefit you and your family. Go back and review that number you originally created in chapter 7. Ask yourself how it would feel to have that exact amount sitting in the bank ready at a moment's notice. No matter what that reason might be, know that the fund is not going to appear overnight, and it's definitely not going to happen without some elbow grease. But knowing the reason will give you the motivation to keep saving.

Commonly Asked Questions

To be honest, perhaps because of my natural tendency to save, I didn't realize how confusing the idea of a fully funded emergency fund was until I started talking about it with others. I've learned that asking someone to save up a significant sum of money is in fact asking a lot. (Remember, I'm married to a Spender.) So let's go through some commonly asked questions about fully funded emergency funds.

Is It Six Months of Income or Six Months of Expenses?

The goal is to save at least six months' worth of living expenses, not income. I know you may push back on this one but hear me out. At this stage in your financial journey—assuming you've paid off all your consumer debts and have freed up your monthly income to go further for you—it's going to be easier and faster to save the amount of your living expenses than your income, and it will also teach you how to get your money to work for you.

With a fully funded emergency fund, you are basically insuring yourself against the loss of income long enough that you can buy yourself some time to land another job or make other dramatic changes in your lifestyle without relying on credit cards or loans to carry you through. It's a form of saving for the future, a financial muscle you need to develop on your way to saving for retirement, the next financial step you will need to tackle. You are giving your family the peace of financial freedom. Later, you will give yourself the gift of financial independence with a beefy retirement account.

Do I Really Need to Save Six Months' Worth of Expenses?

I'm a huge fan of six months versus three or four months. My reasoning is simple: I like security, and having six months' worth of living expenses gives me a number large enough that if we had to run out today to go buy another car in cash, we'd still have enough left over to float us for a few months. Meaning, the larger your emergency fund, the further it can carry you in a pinch.

Is a Roth IRA the Same Thing as an Emergency Fund?

No. A Roth IRA is a retirement investment. It is not intended to save you in an emergency; it is where you purchase investments that will one day fund your retirement. Your emergency fund should be in a *liquid* savings account—where you can access the money quickly without penalty but is siloed from your everyday accounts so you won't dip into it habitually. Your emergency fund is meant to protect your family in the present moment and up to six months, not to live on during your retirement years.

What If I Can't Save That Much Money?

If you find yourself asking this question, let me stop you right here. You can absolutely save that much money. The only person stopping you is you. Like I said, saving money is harder than paying off debt, because you and your family will suffer if you don't pay what you owe others. But there's no bill collector showing up at your door demanding payment if you don't pay yourself. If you want to experience true financial freedom, where you won't be drowning under a mountain of unforeseen expenses, it isn't good enough to just pay off your consumer debt; you also have to build your ark.

Why Build Your Ark?

When the pandemic first hit, I took to social media to tell all my readers that they needed to go into storm mode and start saving as much as they could in case they lost their jobs. Most of my readers appreciated my posts, but a few were not so happy with me. One direct messaged me to say that I was "putting my faith in man instead of God by telling others to aggressively save their money."

I responded to her that even Noah had to build the ark. God did not toss Noah the ark and say, "Hop on, buddy!" No. He told Noah to build the ark, and Noah had to get to work. Noah not only had to put his faith and trust in what the Lord was telling him, but he also had to do the hard, dirty work of building that massive ark. If you are not familiar with the story, Noah didn't build the ark in a day or even a month; it took him *years* to build it. He could have given up at any point, but he didn't. He showed up. He went to work. He built the ark, timber by timber and stick by stick. His neighbors thought he had lost his mind, but when the flood waters came, Noah, his family, and all the animals aboard the ark were safe (Genesis 6–9).

This is what your fully funded emergency fund is supposed to do: keep your family afloat when the flood waters rise. But guess what? Just as God didn't build the ark for Noah, no one else is going to build your emergency fund for you. You have to get to work, laboring to get your family to the place of financial freedom and safety you desire. By now, you've already worked your way toward your starter emergency fund and you've already paid off your consumer debt. So you can achieve this feat! Don't let the naysayer in your head or those around you tell you otherwise.

How to Build Your Ark

The principles behind building up your six-month emergency fund are no different from the principles behind paying off debt or saving up your starter emergency fund. All these steps entail focus and sacrifice. The key is to be sure that you don't allow a certain lifestyle to creep in. It happens when you stop paying attention to your money and instead run wild with the extra money you now have; when you start spending even more money because you think now you have the money to spend, instead of staying focused and putting your money to work for your future self.

If you've built up enough financial discipline that you are not running wild with your newfound extra wiggle room in your budget, this next leg of your journey will move quickly for you. You'll find it easy to direct any extra money you have toward your six-month emergency fund. But if you find yourself getting tired of saving and it's becoming extraordinarily difficult to cut back your spending, you may need to slow down your progress a bit. This would be a good time to check in with your spouse and make adjustments to your budget.

At this point in our journey, Pat was burned out from the strictness of our budget over the last two years and really wanted the freedom to spend money. So, once we were debt free, I budgeted $100 a month that he could spend guilt free. The rest I put toward our six-month emergency fund. If you're questioning why Pat felt this way, keep in mind he gave up the freedom to spend money as he pleased while we were on the debt-free journey. He was also working a job he didn't love but couldn't quit until we had that emergency fund. For him, that $100 was what he needed to stay sane in the moment while still preparing for the future.

No one can tell you how fast or how hard you need to work toward your financial freedom. That's something only you and your spouse can figure out, and if one of you is a saver and the other is a spender, it may take months or even years of discussion before you find compromises you *both* can happily live with. But when you are pulling together instead of fighting each other, you'll go faster and harder than you'd ever believe was possible.

With that in mind, let's look at the steps you should take toward saving for your six-month emergency fund.

Step 1: Set a Target Savings Goal for Every Paycheck

Go back to your quick-start budget and set yourself a goal of how much you want to save from your paycheck. Maybe now that you are consumer-debt free and no longer have to make minimum monthly payments, you decide you can afford to set aside $500 every paycheck. Or maybe, like us, you decide your family needs to have a little breathing room to avoid burnout. So instead of putting the full $500 into your emergency fund, you put in $400 and allow the $100 that is left over to be "fun" money. There's no right or wrong answer to what your target savings goal should be. But you do need to have a target and strive to meet it.

STEP 2: RINSE AND REPEAT

You can quickly get the ball rolling by using some of the tactics you used to pay off debt. Go sell some stuff you don't need. Get a side hustle to bring in extra cash. Take advantage of the incredible apps and places online that help you save money or earn cash back.

My personal longtime favorite is Rakuten Rewards (formerly Ebates), where you earn cash back from your online purchases. It even allows you to earn cash back from purchases you pick up in stores. This works for both food and nonfood purchases. For example, whenever I need to make a purchase from Target or Walmart, I head to Rakuten, then to the desired store's website, make the purchases online, then head to the store to pick them up that same day! I earn cash back, plus I don't have to haul all three of my children into a store and spend an hour trying to find everything I need. Not to mention, I'm not tempted to buy the things I don't need while I'm there!

Then there are apps like Fetch Rewards and Ibotta. These apps allow you to earn cash back that you can redeem for gift cards using your store receipts (even with grocery and fuel purchases). With Ibotta, you can cash out using PayPal, which puts cash right back into your bank account! Fetch Rewards has several options for gift cards that can help stretch your budget even further and also provide some guilt-free treats for yourself, like a pumpkin spice latte from Starbucks. As you build up these rewards, cash them out and throw them into your emergency fund.

Don't lose steam now. You've got this! Financial freedom is getting closer with every step you take.

STEP 3: ADJUST AS NEEDED

If you realize at any point that your target savings goal is too high (or too low), it's totally okay to adjust it as needed. It's okay to throw your bonus into your emergency fund or take your kids to the theme park instead. Yes, focus and discipline are key to achieving anything in life, but know that you have a life to live. I know this step in the game is hard. Saving money is hard. That's why, if you or your spouse starts to feel that burnout feeling and you need to adjust your target savings goal for this pay period, do it. Just don't give up on the goal.

STEP 4: KNOW WHY

The month of October 2019 is one that will forever go down in the Fearon family's history as the craziest, most expensive month of our entire marriage. It started on October 9 when our then twenty-year-old HVAC system died on a humid, 93-degree day. Thankfully, we had our six-month emergency fund at the ready and paid cash to the HVAC man.

Then, the very next week, I walked into our basement laundry room and discovered the floor was wet. At first I thought my washing machine must have leaked again. But at that moment my middle child flushed the toilet and the source of the leak became all too clear. That's right, our septic tank had backed up, flooding our finished laundry room and basement. There went another couple of thousand dollars out of the emergency fund to pay for the septic tank to be pumped and for a new "secondhand" dryer to replace the one that had been destroyed when the water ran down the back while it was running. Thankfully our homeowner's insurance covered the remediation costs of gutting and scrubbing our basement and laundry room.

But this wasn't the end of our saga. Not four days later, when Pat was installing the dryer, he discovered that our electrical panel was hot—so hot he couldn't even touch it. Come to find out, the main electrical line coming into our home had blown. It is by the grace of God that our home didn't burn down. As a result, Pat had to rewire our entire home and we had to live without power for two days.

Needless to say, we put our emergency fund to work that month. But you know what? We avoided having to sink back into debt. And even though that was definitely a very stressful time, it wasn't the end of the world, because we had the cash to pay for the expenses. The freedom from stressing over how we were going to pay for things was beyond words. Your fully funded emergency fund turns a major issue into a hiccup.

It's also amazing how much easier it is to "wheel and deal" when you have cash to pay for things. Our HVAC system would have cost $11,000 if we went with the in-house financing option, but because we paid cash, we paid only $6,500 for a brand-new AC and furnace. We got similar benefits with the septic tank and electrical work. My point is, your emergency fund is not only your safety net; it will give you the peace of mind you need when life goes haywire.

When to Use Your Emergency Fund

Although we talked about this in chapter 7, the question bears repeating: When do you use your emergency fund? Do you use it to pay that unexpected bill you forgot about? Do you use it to buy a new bedroom set for your four-year-old? Do you use it to buy a new-to-you car when yours unexpectedly dies? When we need to determine if an expense is an actual emergency, we ask ourselves two questions.

QUESTION 1: WHAT IS AN ABSOLUTELY NECESSARY EXPENSE?

From the questions above, I would say that only one is an absolutely necessary expense: a new-to-you car when yours is completely done. New bedroom furniture isn't an emergency, nor is an unexpected bill. Most of the time, bills *should* be expected, so an unexpected bill is likely a "budget oops," a mistake we make when we fail to account for an expense we should have been able to foresee. If we adjust our budget and make some temporary sacrifices, we can usually afford to pay the unexpected bill without touching the emergency fund.

Expenses that are absolutely necessary and warrant the use of your emergency fund would be:

- Death or illness of a loved one that prompts immediate travel
- Displacement due to a major loss like a house fire or flooding

- Medical expenses
- Job loss
- Necessary home repairs
- Major car repairs

Expenses that are not absolutely necessary would include:

- Vacations
- Christmas (e.g., gifts, decorations, parties, etc.)
- Starting a business
- Latest technology like an iPhone or Apple watch
- Routine and minor car maintenance

For both vacations and Christmas, you should set up a sinking fund and save a little bit from every paycheck toward these goals. Pat and I also do this for our routine auto maintenance, such as oil changes and tires. We have a separate bank account for each one of our sinking funds, where we hold money to pay for these specific expenses whenever they are needed.

QUESTION 2: WHAT IS A TRULY URGENT NEED?

Something urgent could be the sudden relocation of your job and discovering you need to move within the next month. But simply wanting to relocate would not be considered urgent, since you'd have time to prepare and save for the relocation.

When it comes to using your emergency fund, you need to take the long view. It is meant to be your lifelong safety net. To put the questions another way: Do you really want to put a hole in that net or is this a situation where using it will *prevent* you from free falling to the ground?

Is It Really Financial Freedom?

I believe you achieve financial freedom when you've paid off your consumer debt and have a fully funded six-month emergency fund. Once Pat and I achieved those goals, Pat finally had the freedom to start his own business.

In September 2016, Pat left the corporate world. He celebrated our new financial freedom by taking a couple of weeks off to take our two boys on the most epic father-son camping trip ever. Then he hit the ground running, excited to build his home remodeling business.

To my surprise and delight, I watched as my husband came back to life. His corporate job had drained him, turning him into a shell of the man I married. Now, working in his dream job, he was energized and motivated. Happily, we did not need to touch the emergency fund in those early days of Pat starting his business, and the freedom and security we enjoyed were both amazing and strange. We had spent so many years hustling, counting pennies, and sometimes just holding our breath praying nothing unexpected happened, that being able to breathe again felt new to us.

That feeling is the reason I wrote this book. We noticed that no one else in our life could relate to how we were feeling, and we wanted to show people how to do what we had done so they, too, could feel the same financial freedom. That's not to say we no longer experience money stress, just that now we have real breathing room. We have space to live life in a way that best serves our family. We can take vacations. We can buy our kids that trampoline they wanted. We can even give away a large sum of money to help out a single mom. We have room to say yes to the right opportunities and develop the self-awareness and self-discipline to say no to the wrong ones.

The interesting part of our story is that the income we lived on didn't change. My blog, the business I thought was finally going to take off, didn't. I haven't paid myself from my business in over a year. It's not so much that we achieved this state of financial freedom on an income of $47,000 a year but that our income never changed. We simply learned how to manage our income in a way that blessed our family instead of pulling our family down.

The cold hard truth is that most of us live for vacations. We can't wait to have a few days of freedom from our daily lives. But what would your life look like if you weren't just living for that one- or two-week break from life? What would your life look like if you had the freedom to truly go where God calls you? How many times have you felt as if you were supposed to be going here or doing that but couldn't because of your family's financial situation? Financial freedom not only gives you rest from worry and anxiety, but it also allows you to pursue your dreams. Isn't that the life you want?

Let's Make Some Money Moves

1. Write down why it is important to you and your family that you save up a six-month emergency fund. What does financial freedom look like for you?

2. In chapter 7, you came up with a target goal for your fully funded, six-month emergency fund. Take that number and figure out, using your quick-start budget, how much you could save from every paycheck toward your target goal.

3. Decide on a reward for you and your family once you've achieved this incredible feat. Maybe a dinner out at your favorite restaurant or a visit to your kids' favorite amusement park. Brainstorm with your spouse (and kids if they are old enough) and choose a reward that will keep everyone motivated.

4. Look into other possible money-saving and cash-back resources, like Rakuten or Fetch, to help you stretch your budget even further.

Thirteen

PAYING OFF THE MORTGAGE

On January 19, 2019, we finally crossed our long-awaited finish line. I had just made the final payment on what was supposed to be our thirty-year mortgage. I could no longer hold back the tears as I hung up the phone with Wells Fargo. We were now 100 percent debt free. It all felt so surreal.

At thirty-three and thirty-four years old, while raising three small children and living on $47,000 per year, we had just accomplished something that is typically seen as a "retirement" milestone. Now no one but us owned any of our belongings. To celebrate, I had set aside money in our budget so I could buy a bottle of champagne and even a store-bought cake. (My kids didn't even know you could buy cakes at the store, because

Mom always made them!) What began out of sheer desperation on a spring day in 2013 ended on a cold winter day in 2019.

Only, our journey doesn't stop there—nor does yours. In fact, I don't believe our financial journeys will ever be truly over until the good Lord calls us home. And even then, if we've continued to be good stewards of our finances, the money and the assets we leave behind will continue to bless others for generations to come.

Before that January day in 2019, many people thought Pat and I did not have much money. When they heard we had not eaten out or ordered takeout in six months they thought it was because we couldn't afford it. When they found out we had stayed in a tiny home instead of renting an Airbnb on Tybee Island, Georgia, so we could stick to our $1,000 vacation budget, they believed it was because we were "hard up." What they didn't know was that we decided, shortly after saving our six-month emergency fund, that we were going to pay off the house. We wanted to build even more security and freedom with the money we had coming in. We wanted to take that mortgage payment and do more with it than give it away to Wells Fargo every month.

Why Pay Off the Mortgage Early?

Shortly after paying off our house, Pat and I told one of our friends that we no longer had a mortgage payment, and their response was, "Why would you do that? Now you can't take the tax deduction." I replied with a question of my own: "Do you itemize your deductions or take the standard deduction?" Here's why this question matters. Nearly 80 percent of Americans do not itemize their taxes. This means they are not taking the mortgage deduction, because you can only take it if you itemize.

Another argument I've heard is that if you have a low mortgage rate, you should just keep your mortgage because it's not costing you very much. But most people don't know what TIP is, which stands for total interest percentage. You can usually find it either on page three of your loan documents or page five of your closing disclosure. Here's how it works. Say your mortgage is $300,000 with a 4 percent interest rate on a thirty-year mortgage. Do you know how much that mortgage will cost you if you keep it for all thirty years? $515,608 ($300,000 + $215,608). How? Because with TIP, instead of 4 percent of the loan—which would be $12,000—you're really paying 72 percent (or $215,608). You can find TIP under "total interest paid," using an amortization calculator.[5]

For me personally? I'm not a fan of paying a bank that much money for the privilege of living in my home. Now, maybe it's not a big deal to you, and you have no desire to pay off your home early. That's cool too. However, I want to challenge you to think outside the box a little. We've been conditioned to believe that having a paid-for home is an "old person thing." But, really, it's a huge stepping-stone on the journey toward financial independence. Think about all that you could do today with your mortgage payment, not years from now in your retirement.

The average mortgage payment in the United States is $1,200. Twelve hundred dollars a month could go a long way! What could you do with that kind of money each month? Not only could you save up and pay cash for an incredible vacation for your family, but you could also purchase a truckload of toys for Toys for Tots this Christmas! Let's retrain ourselves to no longer think in terms of payments but in terms of the value of those payments. Consider not only what that money can do for us, but what it can do for our communities as well.

Renting

I know we're talking about mortgages and owning homes outright, but I want to make sure you know that renting is okay. You're not somehow failing in your finances if you're renting instead of owning. There are plenty of times when renting makes more sense. If you're just learning how to manage your money well, it makes perfect sense to rent—after all, if the dishwasher breaks in your rental, it's not on you to fix or replace it. Don't fret if you're renting. I promise, you're not throwing your money away even if some of your friends say you are.

Renting can actually be the wiser choice for some people. You should only buy a house if you plan to live there for at least five years, because it's costly to buy and sell a home. If you are single and just starting out, if your job is uncertain, or if you simply want to keep your options open, renting is likely the better option. Also, in some markets the housing costs are so high that for most people renting is the only option. Finally, if you do not have the time, talent, or interest needed to care for a home, renting will give you the most freedom and flexibility to pursue other interests. I have the built-in benefit of a husband who has the interest and ability to fix up our home. But if HGTV makes your skin crawl and you have no interest in DIY home repairs, you might want to rent instead.

How We Did It

So just how did we pay off the house? Did we win the lottery? Did we follow some guru's complicated scheme? Did we follow the popular biweekly payment method? Nope. In fact, you've already heard our method and it might be kind of boring to hear it again, but then, that's what the journey toward financial freedom generally is: boring. It's not full of glitz and glamour; it's boring. But it's one of the most rewarding journeys you can take.

If you want to pay off your mortgage, be sure to wait until after you have a fully funded emergency fund. Remember, your six-month emergency fund is your first step to walking in financial freedom. Having your home paid off is great. But it's not great if you have to sink back into debt a month after paying it off because your HVAC system dies and you don't have the cash to replace it.

Once Pat and I got serious about tackling the mortgage, we followed a similar pattern we used to pay off our consumer debts and save up our six-month emergency fund. We started by prioritizing our mortgage payoff in our budget. We made sure that every extra dollar we had was being applied to the mortgage.

Before you can tackle paying off your mortgage, you need to know a couple of things. What kind of mortgage do you have? Conventional, interest-only, FHA, VA, or ARM? I will describe each mortgage type later in the chapter. Also, are there any penalties for paying off your mortgage early (usually called prepayment penalties)?

We called our lender, Wells Fargo, when we decided to pay off our mortgage early to check with them to make sure there weren't going to be any surprises. We also made sure we could make as many payments in a given month as we wanted. We aren't fans of letting extra money just sit in our bank account, because it has a tendency to disappear. So we wanted to make sure that when we reviewed our budget for the week and there was extra money left, we could immediately apply it to our mortgage.

And this is exactly what we did. We made additional small payments almost every week. Some weeks we only had an extra twenty dollars and some weeks we had an extra three hundred. But—and this is a big but—you need to make sure that when you make these extra payments, they are going toward the *principal only*. I was able to do that easily online, but you'll need to check with your mortgage provider about the best way to do this.

Robert Kiyosaki, the author of *Rich Dad Poor Dad*, gave a

beautiful description of the word *focus*: "FOCUS: Follow One Course Until Successful."[6] We stayed focused on paying off our mortgage until we achieved our goal. Yes, we still put a small amount into our retirement savings during this time, but while paying off the mortgage our goal wasn't to max out our Roth IRA contributions (because there was no way we could do both). Staying intensely focused on our current goal carried us so much further than trying to do too many things at one time. We also updated our mortgage balance tracker every month; watching that huge number fall gave us even more motivation to achieve our goal.

The last step was getting the payoff statement from our lender. This involved a phone call and a letter in the mail giving us our official payoff balance. This is important. You don't want to just log on to your lender's website and pay the balance that's there, because the interest may not have been calculated on that balance yet. If you fail to get an official payoff balance from the bank, guess what you're going to get in the mail next month? Another bill for your house. Make sure to call and get your payoff statement before you make your final payment.

Where Did the Money Come From?

Shortly after paying off our home we were hanging out at a friend's house with a group of people we had not previously met. Our mutual friend told this new group of folks that we had paid off our house. The guy sitting to my right leaned over and said, "Congratulations, that's awesome! So how much do your parents give you guys every month to live on?"

Offended by his question, my husband immediately replied, "Our parents have never given us money."

Confused, the guy went on to ask, "I mean, you guys have kids, so how did you pay off the house and afford to live?"

His question awoke something in me because this guy was thirty-nine years old. He was almost seven years older than me and still relied on his parents to help him pay for his rent! He had no children, and he was terrified to marry his longtime girlfriend because he didn't think they could live without his parents' help. Not only that, but when I scanned the room, I realized Pat and I were the only ones in the group who didn't receive money from our parents.

Now, before you think I'm judging, I'm not. My concern was that no one—not even our mutual friend whose house we were in—knew how to survive without their parents' help. And we were in a room full of thirtysomethings! What are they going to do when their parents are no longer here on earth to support them financially?

Did we receive money from family? The answer is no. The money to pay off our forty-year-old home came from Pat and me. Sure, the twenty dollars my mom gave me on my birthday went toward paying the mortgage. (Sorry, Mom!) But she certainly didn't give us money specifically to pay a debt. We threw every little bit of extra money we had at the mortgage and we side hustled. Pat built cabinets and did handyman stuff on the side, and I wrote freelance articles and tutored college students online.

There's no big secret to paying off your mortgage. It's not easy, but it's worth it. It's different when you own your home. It's a little strange to no longer be making payments to live somewhere. I had been paying either rent or a mortgage since I was eighteen years old, so it took some time to get used to seeing the old mortgage payments move into savings instead of out the door every month.

Since we no longer have mortgage payments, we've been able to max out our Roth IRA contributions, and we've even been able to give in ways we never dreamed possible. But maybe you're just getting started in the world of home ownership and you're baffled by the whole process. Before I talk more about paying off the mortgage, let's dive into the process of actually *getting* a mortgage.

How Much House Can I Afford?

I don't know that there's anything more stressful or confusing than buying a house, and I've only done it once! There were so many things I didn't understand, like the debt-to-income ratio and how my student loans (which were not going to be called due for another year) almost destroyed our shot at getting a mortgage. I didn't understand why the bank wouldn't let us put the full amount we had saved as a down payment on the house. Everything was confusing, and our broker even said to me, "Don't try to understand it, because you won't ever get it."

Well, that dear sir apparently had never met a Southern woman, because I took his statement as a challenge. Now I can confidently say that I finally understand this home-buying process—or at least enough that if we were to do it again, I would be way more prepared. I could write a whole other book on the process, so I'm just going to hit the high notes—the things you definitely need to know before starting.

First, you need to determine how much house you can afford, since that number will shape your house hunt. Most experts say you should never take on a mortgage where the payment will be more than 30 percent of your take-home pay. But I believe it should be considerably lower than that. In addition, you will need to factor in the cost of home insurance and real estate taxes. Bankrate.com has an excellent mortgage calculator where you can start plugging in numbers to get a sense for how much house you can afford.

I have one big caution, though. Calculators on financial websites rarely include the costs of renovating, repairing, and maintaining a home. You'll need to keep these potential costs in mind even if you purchase a newly built home.

How Do I Qualify for a Mortgage?

When it comes to buying your first home, debt matters. This is why it's important to be as close to consumer-debt free as possible before you purchase a home. When you apply for a mortgage, someone you have never met will be digging deep into your financial life and finding every single mistake you've ever made with money. Therefore, before you begin the home-buying process, pull your credit report and go through it with a fine-tooth comb. (You can do this for free from all three credit bureaus at annual creditreport.com.) If you find any errors, report them to the bureaus and get them corrected. That way you will know your mortgage originator is working with an accurate credit history.

Along with making sure your credit report is accurate, you need to make sure you have adequate savings. How much do you want to put down on a home? The recommended amount is 20 percent of the purchase price, since that helps you avoid the extra cost of having private mortgage insurance (PMI) tacked on to your mortgage. A 20 percent down payment also qualifies you for a conventional mortgage, which will usually give you a better interest rate.

I'll explain more about the different types of mortgages in a moment, but for now, decide how much you want to save as your down payment—which cannot be all the money in your savings account. You'll need to have your down payment plus money left over in your savings account. That's why your down payment should not be taken out of your emergency fund. Remember, your emergency fund is for emergencies only—not for taking on the largest debt of your life.

Types of Home Loans

Understanding the type of mortgage you have can help you navigate how to pay it off. Not every mortgage is great. If you have one that's less than ideal, it may make more sense to refinance your current mortgage into a better one first. But I would add this caution if you are considering refinancing: it isn't free. Refinancing typically costs anywhere between $3,000 to $6,000. Before you refinance, you need to figure out whether it makes sense to fork over that kind of money.

If you're a first-time home buyer, don't allow a mortgage broker to sell you a mortgage you cannot afford. Do your own research and run your own numbers with a free online calculator before you sign on the dotted line.

Now let's take a look at the various loan types out there, from the worst to the best.

ADJUSTABLE-RATE MORTGAGES (ARMs)

Basically, with an ARM, you start with a lower interest rate that increases as the loan matures. The thought process (and how this mortgage is typically marketed) is that you begin with the lower interest rate while you're just starting out in your career. Then, by the time the higher interest rate kicks in, you would have achieved a better paying job and therefore can afford more. The concept of the ARM is to transfer the risk of potential higher interest rates to the borrower.

Here's the deal: if you're offered one of these mortgages, please run the opposite way. These are notoriously bad mortgages because the payments will rise so substantially that they can and do financially cripple folks. You also don't have a crystal ball, and there's no way for you to know for sure that you'll make more money in five or seven years. As the pandemic has taught all of us, we can't make assumptions about our future.

INTEREST-ONLY

Honestly, I don't even know why these exist, because you're only paying the interest. You're basically throwing money away. You're not going to be making any headway on your principal balance. I mean, isn't the point to one day own your home outright? If so, avoid this loan. And if you currently have one, please look into refinancing it into a better mortgage option. Otherwise, you may want to rent.

FEDERAL HOUSING ADMINISTRATION (FHA)

These loans are insured by the US Department of Housing and Urban Development (HUD) and typically marketed to first-time home buyers. This is the mortgage we had on our home. With an FHA loan, you can put down as little as 3.5 percent, but that means you will have private mortgage insurance added to your mortgage (more on PMI below). These loans are typically offered at only thirty years, but I have heard that some brokers will offer a fifteen-year option.

Veterans Affairs (VA)

These loans are insured by the US Department of Veterans Affairs and only offered to service members. Some VA loans will allow you to purchase a home with no or a very small down payment. The biggest downside to these loans is the one-time funding fee, which is based on how much money you're putting down, how long you have served, and if this is your first, second, or third VA loan.

Conventional

These types of loans are the most well-known because they have been around the longest. They are also one of the best options. Conventional loans are not backed by the government, like the FHA or VA loans, but instead are privately insured against default. You will need to put down at least 10 percent of the home sale price for this loan. However, you'll need to put down at least 20 percent to avoid PMI. You can finance them for fifteen or thirty years.

Other Important Terms

When it comes to buying a house, you'll need to know the meaning of a few other terms that get tossed around.

Private Mortgage Insurance (PMI)

This is not a mortgage loan. It is something that you will come across if you put down less than 20 percent of the price of the home. Trust me when I tell you it's a huge pain in the neck to get rid of. It's not impossible, but you will need to pay this along with your regular mortgage payment every month until you have paid at least 80 percent of the principal on your mortgage. Some mortgage companies also have other stipulations that must be met before PMI can come off. Wells Fargo required that we not only pay down the mortgage balance by 20 percent but also carry the mortgage for at least five years.

Here's why doing your own math is important. When we first called to get the PMI removed and found out we couldn't because it had not yet been five years since getting the mortgage, we were told to refinance. When Pat and I looked at the numbers, we realized that refinancing our home would cost us $3,500 in fees but keeping the PMI until the five-year time limit was up would cost us only $700. For obvious reasons, we decided to just keep the PMI instead of refinancing. Always do your own math.

Escrow

This is an account that will house money to pay for your home insurance premiums and property taxes every year. It can house other expenses, but these two are the most common. Escrow will be included in your monthly mortgage payment at most financial institutions, but some smaller banks may have this as a separate payment. It does not get applied to interest or the principal balance. It acts like a savings account (but it isn't); the money you pay into escrow from your mortgage payment every month goes toward paying for the abovementioned expenses. When you pay off the mortgage, whatever balance is in escrow will be refunded to you.

CLOSING COSTS

These are the expenses you'll have to pay at closing when you're purchasing your home. They can include the home inspection bill, appraisal fee, premium fee for homeowner's insurance, attorney expenses, credit report charges (where they paid to pull your credit report), title search, loan origination fees, and so on. Keep in mind that some of these fees will need to be paid before the actual closing on the property, such as earnest money (also known as a good-faith deposit, the amount you put down to show you're serious about purchasing the home; this is not to be confused with your overall down payment) and the fee for the home inspection.

If you're a buyer, you should be prepared to pay around 3 to 4 percent of the home's purchase price in closing costs. If you're a seller, count on paying around 1 to 3 percent of the sale price of your home.[7]

How to Make a Plan to Pay Off the House

Have you ever heard of an amortization table? This is sometimes called an amortization schedule. If not, it can be your best friend at figuring out how to pay off a large debt fast. An amortization table lays out how each one of your payments (with your interest rate calculated) affects the overall principal of your mortgage. For a thirty-year mortgage your amortization schedule would show 360 payments total. If you're looking to pay off your mortgage early, pull up a free online amortization calculator and start playing around with the numbers. Let's say that instead of paying off your mortgage in thirty years you want to pay it off in ten years. You would change the loan term length from thirty to ten, and that will give you the new monthly payments you should be making on your mortgage.

That new monthly payment number may look scary, but it's not. It's information. You now know what your goal should be in order to pay off your mortgage in ten years. For example, let's say you have a starting mortgage balance of $300,000 with a monthly payment of roughly $1,564 at a 4.75 percent interest rate. You've been in your home for five years, but you want to have it paid off in the next ten years. Your new monthly payment amount would be roughly $3,145 a month.

Here's the beauty of knowing that number: you now have a target to hit. You know how much it's going to take every month to pay off your mortgage in the time frame you want— even if that number doesn't appear doable. When Pat and I first did this exercise, our number didn't seem doable either.

There's no hard and fast rule that you absolutely must pay this new amount every month or else you must go back to the thirty-year mortgage. All this number does is give you a working target to strive for. You now know how much extra money you need to find in your budget or how much extra side work you need to do. You know how helpful it will be to throw that Christmas bonus at the mortgage instead of going on a shopping spree. Math is your friend when it comes to managing your money. Information is good, because it gives you the freedom to make decisions that are right for your family. Maybe when you see that new number you'll realize that although you do want to pay off the mortgage early, you also need to be saving for retirement and would like to take a family vacation at least every other year. Maybe you'll realize, yes, we would love to have the house paid for in ten years, but maybe fifteen years is more doable with our current season of life.

Remember, there is nothing wrong with doing what works best for your family. Just because my family paid off our home quickly doesn't mean you have to. We bought our home as a foreclosure and therefore had a much smaller starting mortgage than $300,000. If you're working with a higher mortgage, it may take you longer to pay it off. But in the end, no matter how long it takes, you will own your home outright! So what if it takes you longer than you planned? You still achieved a feat most people can't even imagine.

Choosing Your Next Big Goal

I'll be honest, even paying off our mortgage didn't give us full financial independence. Technically, you are only financially independent when you are able to live off your investments. In other words, you are financially independent only when your money is working for you, instead of you working for your money. Most people achieve this goal at retirement. That's why Pat's and my next financial goal is saving and investing for retirement, so when we are old and unable to work, our investments will generate enough income for us to live on.

With each financial goal you achieve—paying off debt, creating an emergency fund, owning your home outright—you'll eventually need to take another financial step. It's like finally climbing over the edge of a cliff. You're safe, but you're only safe for so long. You'll eventually have to continue moving forward to keep and maintain your newfound financial freedom. If you don't, you will risk falling off the cliff again.

Our next step is to max out our Roth IRA contributions. What is your next step? Are you saving for a down payment on your dream home or hoping to pay off your mortgage early? Once you are consumer-debt free and have a fully funded six-month emergency fund, the possible financial pathways start to change a little. You now have the freedom to choose where you take your finances next. Chances are, what you do next will be different from what we did. But, nevertheless, I have no doubt you're going to achieve magnificent things, because you've already done the hard work of getting good with your money.

Let's Make Some Money Moves

1. If you plan to purchase a home, find out how much house you can afford. Decide on a goal for your down payment and pull your credit report to correct any errors before you apply for a loan.

2. If your goal is to outright own your home early, pull up a free amortization calculator online and determine how much extra money you'll need to throw at your mortgage to achieve your new payoff timeline. Review the terms of your loan to learn how to pay it off without a prepayment penalty.

3. What is your next money goal? As you achieve each financial goal, write down a new goal and move forward. Keep taking steps to make positive changes in your family's finances.

CONCLUSION

This isn't the end of your story. It's just the beginning.

Maybe when you started this book you were like me on that spring day in 2013—afraid, confused, and without a clue as to what our next right financial move should be. I've shared my family's story so you can hopefully see that, yes, it is possible to achieve your own version of financial freedom regardless of your past mistakes. The peace that comes from that freedom is incredible, and my prayer is that throughout our walk together in these pages, you've discovered it is possible for you too. No matter your life circumstances, you can also achieve your own version of financial freedom. I have no doubt that your version will be different from ours, and that is so beautiful.

I know that changing your life for the better can be challenging, whether you're single, married, or divorced, or whether or not you have children. Doing something new can be daunting. But, dear friend, you've got this. Getting good with money isn't for the faint of heart, and you've proven that you're up for the challenge. Use the road map laid out for you in this book and work to apply it to your real life.

Personal finance is just that. Personal. And that's what makes it so amazing. You get to decide how you'll use your income and how you'll make positive changes, not only in your own life but also in your community. Learn from others, be inspired, but then guiltlessly do what works best for you and your family and what will bring you closer to your goals of financial freedom.

If you're a parent, I hope you'll bring your children along on this journey with you. Give them the gift of seeing you work hard toward making positive changes. It will stir within them the courage to make changes as they grow.

If you're waiting for permission to start, here it is: My dear friend, start your own amazing journey toward financial freedom and beyond. Go make those money moves. You've got this. Your future self will thank you!

ACKNOWLEDGMENTS

While my name may be on the cover, this book would not have happened without an army of people guiding me and challenging me. There were so many wonderful souls who helped me get this project off the ground.

My business coach, Alli: your invaluable advice helped me find the courage to write out my book proposal. My friend and fellow author, Brittany Ann, thank you for being willing to walk beside me and help me navigate the world of book writing. Fellow bloggers and authors, Erin and Crystal, thank you both so much for your guidance in navigating the world of literary agents and proposal writing. My amazing friend, Catherine Alford, thank you so much for your texts that encouraged me when writing got tough. Stacey, thank you for being the first set of eyes on my book and helping me shape it into the best rough draft possible. My literary agent, Teresa, I'm pretty sure

I hit the jackpot! Thank you for being a guiding light and going to bat for me!

My team at Nelson Books, thank you for all the hand holding and guidance in launching my first book!

My blog readers, what started out as a small diary sharing the nuances of our family's money journey turned into a wonderful community of people I can't imagine living life without. Thank you for showing up every day and blessing me with your kindness and encouragement. The world needs more beautiful souls like you online!

A very special thank-you to my FIA sisters who prayed over me and this book: Kodak, Mama Bear, Fonda, Stitch, Seinfeld, Sugar Mama, Canon, Paperback, and Homeland. Thank you for your prayers, encouragement, and support. I'm forever grateful that God placed you all in my life!

My hometown friends, Lindz, Meg, Jesseca, Shannon, Karen, Morgan, Kristy, Brittany, and Yajaira, for always believing in me and being my very first blog readers! Your love and support have carried me through so much.

My incredible husband, Pat. Without your support and encouragement, I would have never typed the first word. Thank you, babe, for always pushing me out of my comfort zone and being willing to jump in the deep end with me. Your willingness to do whatever it takes is the reason we've been able to do so much. You're my favorite part of life!

And there's no doubt that this book would look very different if it weren't for the three beautiful souls entrusted to Pat and me. Conner, Collin, and Charlotte, you three are beyond blessings to me. Thank you for being willing to give Mommy the space she needed to work on this project. And thank you for cheering me on when I was struggling to find the words to write.

My heavenly Father, thank you for the beautiful gift of writing and for giving me the courage to write our story to share with others. I pray that I have served you well.

Notes

1. Lindsay Frankel, "How to Handle Financial Infidelity in Your Relationship," MagnifyMoney, September 19, 2019, https://www.magnifymoney.com/blog/banking/financial-infidelity/.
2. "What Percentage of Millennials Have Student Debt," *California Business Journal*, July 12, 2021, https://calbizjournal.com/what-percentage-of-millennials-have-student-debt.
3. Marcel Schwantes, "15 Kobe Bryant Quotes from His Legendary Career That Will Inspire You," January 26, 2020, *Inc.*, https://www.inc.com/marcel-schwantes/15-kobe-bryant-quotes-from-his-legendary-career-that-will-inspire-you.html.
4. Dave Ramsey, "What Is a FICO Score and How Does It Work?" Ramsey Solutions, April 27, 2021, https://ramseysolutions.com/debt/what-is-a-fico-score.
5. You can find many free amortization calculators online. For example, Bankrate.com has a fantastic one that is very user-friendly at https://www.bankrate.com/calculators/mortgages/amortization-calculator.aspx.

6. Robert Kiyosaki, *Rich Dad Poor Dad*, twentieth anniversary edition (Cleveland, OH: Plata Publishing, 2017), 253.
7. Judy Dutton, "How Much Are Closing Costs? Plus: How to Reduce Closing Costs," Realtor.com, August 20, 2020, https://www.realtor.com/advice/buy/reduce-closing-costs/.

About the Author

Jessi Fearon is a personal finance writer and coach who seeks to challenge, encourage, and equip women to take the steps they need to achieve financial freedom. Jessi firmly believes in living a real life on a budget and that personal finance is, in fact, personal. She seeks to help others learn how to make their money work for them. Jessi has written guest posts for popular websites such as RamseySolutions.com, MSN Money, MoneySavingMom.com, Clark.com, TheHumbledHomemaker .com, Popsugar.com, and HuffingtonPost.com. She and her family make their home in the Atlanta area.

She would love to stay in touch with readers through her blog (jessifearon.com) or on social media (@jessifearon), where she posts regularly on everything life and money. Her passion is to help others realize their own potential through defining their own version of financial freedom.